Blood On The Ceiling:

The Awesome Calamities of Addiction And The Miracle of Recovery

By Nelson Trout

Goodnight Kiss Publishing, Hollywood, California
© 2012

Blood On The Ceiling:
The Awesome Calamities of Addiction
And The Miracle of Recovery

Second Edition

Written by Nelson Trout

Published by:
Goodnight Kiss Publishing
10153 ½ Riverside Dr., #239
Toluca Lake, CA 91602
(808) 331-0707

Edited by Todd Levow
Front cover photograph and cover art by Marjie Parsons
Back cover photograph by Nick Troolin

Printed in the United States of America

Library of Congress Control Number: 2012930153
Trout, Nelson
        Blood On The Ceiling:
        The Awesome Calamities of Addiction
        And The Miracle of Recovery

    p.   cm.
ISBN 978-0-9703563-5-2
        1.   Addiction
        2.   Self Help
        3.   Alcoholism
        4.   Drug Rehab

© 2012 Goodnight Kiss Publishing

DEDICATION

Lovingly dedicated to God and my family

Special thanks to Todd Levow for his friendship, hard work and expertise

Table of Contents

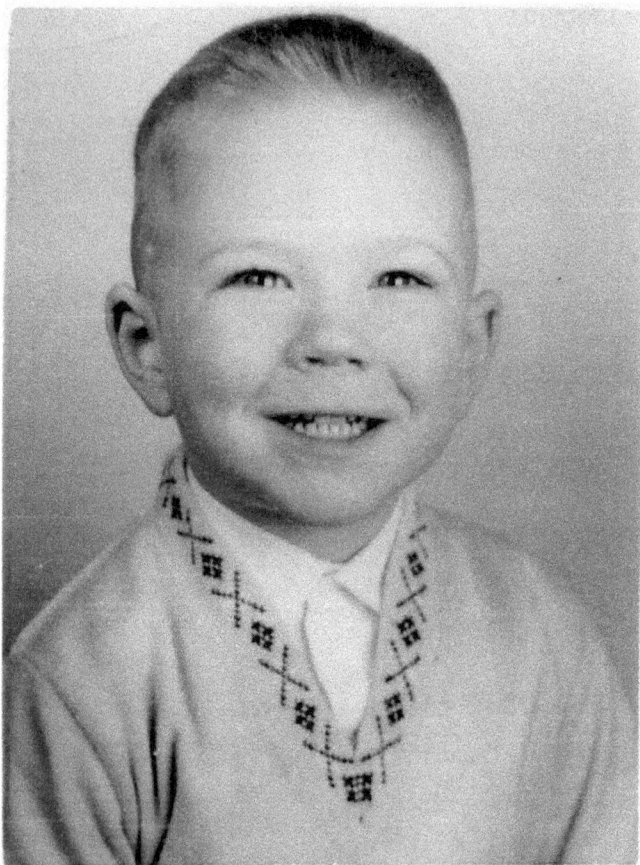

CULVER SCHOOL
1959

"We all start out so innocent"

FLIGHT 265

The soft glow of

A dream never dreamt

The excitement of wisdom

Never sought in this dimension-

Recovery from addiction

Is bold

Like a calvary of warmth

Moving in against the cold.

Somewhere over the Atlantic Ocean at 37,000 Feet September 17th, 2009.

Preface

...Sometimes We Must Stand Alone...

My name is Nelson. I am a recovering alcoholic and drug addict. I drank and used for over 30 years to some degree or another.

During those years I raised a family, held good jobs, owned a home, and coached baseball and softball. I never missed any of my daughter's gymnastic meets. I always got my son to his guitar lessons and proudly attended all of his performances. I have written more than 300 songs, one of which ("New Jersey USA") is a State Song of New Jersey and ("More To Offer") which is the official song of the county of Cumberland in New Jersey where I grew up. I've also released 4 CDs of original music. Both of my children are college graduates and are very successful. My grandson is more precious to me than words can describe. My Sunshine!

I have always deeply loved and admired my wife Susan. I still do and probably always will. She never liked it, but I called her my "hero" (sorry Hon, but it was true). I never cheated on her or physically abused her, though I have verbally abused her in the past, and of that I am deeply ashamed. There were times when I was under the influence that I would lash out at Susan in my frustration and pain. She was the nearest available target. Like the song says, "You Always Hurt The One You Love."

On May 25th, 2009, after an argument, I stood in Susan's dressing room holding our beloved black Pomeranian, Coco, and watched her pack her two suitcases and leave. My world suddenly crashed down around me. The pain of that night was too intense for tears, and I knew it was nearly entirely all my fault.

After three months of my self induced, secluded hell on earth, on September 2nd, 2009, I made the decision to check myself into rehab in New Jersey to help save my marriage and my life. My therapist there diagnosed my dilemma as the disease of alcoholism and drug addiction, fueled by a troubled childhood, mostly having to do with the relationship between my father and myself. Fifty years of hurt. Yet, I never thought I would ever reach the point when I had to admit to myself, my family and my God that I had a problem. A frightful disease I soon learned could only be cured by total abstinence from all mood altering substances, alcohol and drugs alike, and the fellowships of Alcoholics Anonymous and Narcotics Anonymous. It was not an easy thing to do, I must tell you.

Yet my story is quite simple and all too common. As I mentioned, I had always had a taste for alcohol and anything else, depending on the circumstances, that could give me a little buzz. You know, laugh a little harder, create a little more deeply, and block out the never ending hurt while keeping everything under control, for the most part, that is.

On January 13, 2009, I had an accident at work, severely injuring my lower back, fracturing three vertebra in my neck and lacerating the back of my head, which was difficult to close and required twelve stitches and two doctors before it was all over.

Bloody mess. I feel the need here to say that I was completely sober and straight when the accident occurred.

Long story short, the pain was so bad that I was prescribed narcotics. I was also getting depressed and anxious about my physical condition, especially the pain and my limited mobility (which I was told may never go away), my back and neck pain were so severe that my doctors prescribed Oxycodone to cope with the hurt and Xanax to relieve the anxiety and depression brought on by the pain and my new lack of mobility which had been such a big part of my life, as I had always been a very active person.

On top of that, my taste for beer and wine increased and I was using the alcohol to self medicate. Booze and pills - a wicked combination. Believe me!

I had run into the brick wall of dependency. By the time I hit that wall, the disease of addiction had already grown roots in my body, mind and spirit. Like a cancer, it kept growing. I found that out the hard way when I decided to get myself into treatment and end this nightmare which had ensnared me and changed my personality to quite a degree. I became somewhat of a hermit and was not the man, husband, or father that I had been.

Nonetheless, I have a beautiful, healthy family and good friends of which I am proud and forever thankful. I am no longer the man other people expect me to be nor am I the same man I used to be, and though that can be a double edged sword, I am comfortable with who I am and the path I am taking.

This inside look into addiction and recovery contains some of the shocking stories related to me while spending time in two separate rehabs, countless AA and NA meetings, and four months in a halfway house during my journey of withdrawal and early recovery, and of the inspiring people I've met along the way. This book is not only a peek into my diary, but many others' intimate and death defying adventures as well.

To the best of my knowledge every word in this book is true. For anonymity's sake, which is the 12th tradition of NA and AA, all names and locations have been changed. Please prepare yourself, as some of these stories that you are about to read are no less than unsettling, to say the least, and NOT for the faint of heart.

However, please keep in mind that these are just ordinary people, like you and me. The rich, the poor and the in between. Plain folks from every walk of life imaginable who have been cursed with a condition that is ruthless and heartless. These stories illustrate not only their despair and struggles, but their successes too, at overcoming a monster so awful few can imagine the power in its ferocity and strength.

Awesome calamities. Awesome human beings!

Nelson John Trout

"In the backyard of my grandparent's farmhouse.
Still innocent" – 1961

PART I: REHAB

Suffering is truly a test of faith. Those silent, lonely hours when you have no one else but God, makes one tough in mind, body and spirit. And desperation is revealed, almost magically, for what it is - a gift.

12:00 am, October 10, 2009

Day 1

*"I had no idea what to expect when I arrived in Florida.
Everything happened so quickly. I didn't even know I was
coming down here until yesterday. The plane ride was
surreal. I was in an emotional hurricane with no other
option but to look at the clouds and give in to the wind.
Hello, goodbye."*

Flew in from Atlantic City to another rehab near Fort Lauderdale.
Nice place; pool – ocean. Got checked in. Took piss test. Ron, a
tech in his late 60's, and a former crackhead, took Russ, who I
flew down with, and I to the store for grocery shopping. Got into
my apartment. Met my room-mates Mark and Patrick. Seemed like
good guys. Went to bed and read "Shutter Island" by Dennis
LaHane. Went to sleep. Great book by the way.

Russ, 25 and a law school student, had been booting heroin for a
few years. Could even shoot the juice while he was driving. A real
pro! Good kid with a big heart. Wants to get clean. We did 14 days
together at a New Jersey rehab. Detoxed there together. Rough.

Randolph, a garbage head and pyromaniac has been here a few
days. Also from the New Jersey rehab. He said somebody stole a
gallon of milk out of his fridge and not to trust anyone.

Seems Patrick's dad was hard on him, and now he is hard on his
own kid who turns 18 tomorrow, Patrick told me through tears.
Those childhood memories drove Patrick to a ½ gallon of Captain
Morgan's Rum a day. Too much. It was killing him so now he's

here. He's tired of taking out the rage of his childhood on his own son with the help of The Captain.

Day 2

"Just another leg of the journey I never expected to take. Gonna have to be tough, I can see that. The staff and therapists here are fantastic human beings, though. A soft cushion to land on after a rock hard fall."

Got up at 6:30am, went down to the picnic tables for coffee and a smoke. The four wooden tables are laid out side by side in a long row, with benches on each side under a canopy for protection from the rain and the often brutal sun. The hangout for us "clients", so to speak.

Still dark. Nobody there except a guy named Jon, from Oregon. I saw him do a double take on me. He came over looking at me hard, like he was in shock or something or wanted to fight. I was instantly ready. He pulled out a Newport, bummed a light and said I looked exactly like his older brother. I said, "Poor fuckin' guy." He didn't laugh.

Then he said that his brother Steve had just died in April and it really bummed me out. I said I'm sorry and we had coffee and smokes together. Very nice guy. Jon is a diabetic and slams meth.

When Mark wakes up I'm gonna ask him to shave my hair off. He's got clippers. Patrick told me that earlier. Shaky today, but it's early yet.

Met Spike, record producer for Brittney Spears, Back Street Boys – Nashville and New York. Cool, but scared and troubled. Always shaking.

First day in my primary group and a woman named Reagan stood up and said she was leaving, but she doesn't remember why or where she's going.

Wow, I'm thinking, what a fuckin' place!

Salena, also in our group of eight was sharp as hell, and the major drug distributor for several counties in upper New York State. Learned a lot of incredible things about Salena as time went on. You'll see.

Cindy, another member of our group, told us while crying, that she OD'd on heroin and had to be resuscitated with a defibrillator. That's when her mom figured out she was a junkie.

Marcus played football for the University of Pittsburgh. Heroin addict.

Paul from Michigan's nephew died last night. OD'd on heroin. Blames himself. First one to get his nephew partyin'.

Crying in session.

Marcus's brother died last week. Same deal. You get hardened to this shit in a hurry and count your blessings. Sad realities. Life is tough sometimes, man. Stop trying to control it, just gotta go with the flow and do the next right thing.

In group this afternoon, Mike said he was all fucked up on cheap vodka and oxys driving his pick-up truck when his aunt, who is psychic, called his mom to say she thought Mike was gonna have an accident. Two minutes later he hit a tree and ripped his nose off and ruptured his spleen.

David turned an atheist surgeon into a true believer. Deeply stabbed 7 times, the doctor said there was no way he could live. He did. The Doc now believes in God and miracles.

Joe, an old junkie, was shot 5 times in the lower abdomen. His vital organs were miraculously spared. Higher Power, dude.

Young Jeff who is still detoxing and getting chemo for lymphoma, turned up dirty for heroin in a surprise piss test.

He asked Alice if she wanted some. Hard as it was, she said no. Her arms sprinkled with ugly track marks, says she'll die if she shoots again. Talks a lot. Smart, witty like most addicts. Still struggling with the monster, the Devil. Alice is a beautiful person with a gorgeous face and smile.

When I first got here I signed up for the Christian path of recovery. Great move. We went to church tonight. Very cool!

Talked to Jay for a while at the picnic tables. He's 24 and a paramedic from North Carolina. For the last 3 years he'd been doing/snorting 15 40mg oxy's a day. His grandmother OD'd on heroin when his dad was 17. His dad is a hard core alcoholic. He gets this disease honestly. That's for damn sure.

Jay's here because he couldn't live like that anymore. Had to be taped down while detoxing. Hope he makes it. Good kid. Cool accent. Big dude. Must've been strong ass tape.

Just found out Russ had to be put in restraints too, as I should've been on September 3rd.

Worst day of my life. I was up in the South Jersey rehab, withdrawing from booze, percs, zannys and pot. For a little over two days my entire body was screaming in pain and I was hallucinating. The nurses kept a good eye on me and kept injecting me in the ass with anti-seizure medication. I didn't know that combo was a worse detox than heroin. You learn a lot. Back and neck hurt like hell.

Feels good to FEEL, though. No narcotic pain killers needed thank you very much, no matter how bad I hurt!

In 50 minutes I'm gonna go down to the tables and have a smoke. That'll be midnight.

I was in the pool today. Felt great, but killed my back later.

Alice is so funny, she never shuts up. Always something cool to say, though. 3rd day in a row they piss tested her. So far she's clean.

Oh yeah, Laura, a lady at the church, gave me a new bible and wrote a bunch of stuff in the front. She said it's all about Him. Cool band at the church. We all sang along.

Mario, from New Mexico bummed an apple flavored black & mild cigar off me after church. Said he is a song-writer. Wrote 1 fuckin' song. I didn't say shit. Didn't want to hurt his feelings, since I had written 300 plus. Later though, he wrote his 2nd song, it was about addiction. It's a great song and I was really happy for him when he performed it in big-group the next morning. Hard core tequila drinker. Drummer for 35 years. Nice guy. He was at church too.

Somebody said that religion is for those who are afraid to go to hell and spirituality is for those who've been there. Made sense to me. I've become quite spiritual you might say. Yeah, works for me!

Just wrote a postcard for my grandson, Carter. I miss him.

Almost 2am.

Day 3

> *"Time to face another day. Not giving myself a chance to miss home. There is really nothing I can do about it right now anyway. Just gotta have faith in myself and God. Hope I'm a strong enough for all this shit."*

7:42am. Was just gonna go down to the tables, and my new roommate Ricky walks into our two-bed bedroom. Gonna go down and have a smoke and a cup of coffee. I'll check Ricky out later and let you know what he's all about.

Read my daily meditation about letting go and letting God. Good thing to read every day. Thanks' Kim!

OK, Ricky is sitting across from me now, doesn't know I'm writing about him. Little black guy from St. Thomas. Very bad alcoholic. 42 and works in education. Brandy man. Hard to understand when he talks, but that's okay.

Just got back from the gym. Tried to pump some light iron dumbbells but my back couldn't take it, and I ended up in the jacuzzi with Layla from St. Croix.

Some dude threw a padlock on mine and Randolph's locker we shared in the locker room that day. Had to be cut off with bolt cutters by one of the gym workers because they couldn't find the guy who did it. Big ass gym. Huge. Jimmy from Jersey got royally pissed off because a tech screamed at him when he went out in front of the gym and lit up a cigarette.

When we got back to the tables I got talking to this guy Pat who had just lost his football scholarship at Baltimore State in Maryland. Huge running back with a bad oxy habit. Been here 90 days already. He's broken almost every bone in his body. A little pissed off at himself for smoking Marlboro's again. Seems to be a common thing around here. Oxy's are murder. A thousand bucks a week to support his habit. Pat fell hard in detox. Suffered like hell. That little pill chewed him up and spit him out.

Just met Rex from Rhode Island and April from Toronto, both in their early 20's. Both hard core alcoholics. April would hide in her closet and drink vodka from the bottle. Nobody knew she was there. Except her. Addiction can be a frightening, lonely world.

Alice was telling some wild ass grotesque stories again about a box cutter fight with 7 of her friends. She got sliced real bad and lost a lot of blood, but the dragon was roaring, and she didn't give a fuck. Long, deep scar to go along with all the skin picking scars.

She also told how she once got a clot stuck in her needle while shooting up. She pulled the needle out of one of the last good veins in her left arm, pointed it toward the sky, and pushed the plunger. Hard. When the clot broke through the tip of the syringe, it squirted out blood on the ceiling of her bedroom, up above and in between the ceiling fan blades. Her parents still haven't seen it.

She wiped the blood off of her walls, but said, "Fuck the ceiling, too high to reach." She says, "I used to push those clots through, baby."

Big black Raymond from Wilmington, Delaware is a diehard coke freak. Just coke and ice water and cigarettes. When he was thirteen he came home and found his mom in bed with another man while his dad was at work.

Young David freaked out. When he was about 30 he caught his wife in bed with his brother. Real trigger, and his disease really kicked into overdrive.

He's the best damn singer I ever heard. He and I did a duet of "You've Lost That Lovin' Feeling" by the Righteous Brothers for the other freaks out at the tables. We both had a good time and we got an ovation from everyone, but we both have lost that lovin' feeling.

For now. For sure.

Then we sat down, had a smoke, and bullshitted.

I went to church again. Awesome!

Oh yeah, David had a shiny gold front tooth. The late Luther Vandross's 2nd cousin, he sang with Luther at a couple of family picnics till the coke beat his brains in, along with all the heartbreaks.

Nikki, 49, has a cool Brooklyn accent. NYC policewoman for 20 years. On the scene at ground zero on 9/11. Lost 3 friends in the towers that day. She watched people jump out the windows. Felt helpless. Nothing she could do. Retired 3 years ago, and her new job was knockin' back a 30 pack of beer a day. Kinda' cute, in her own sassy way. Needs help to quit.

Russ chimed in and said that he tried to strangle his mother from behind, so she reached around and stabbed him deep in the back with a pencil. He showed us his scar.

My buddy Jon, dead Steve's brother, in a special group meeting, told about his 3 bouts of pancreatitis. The last one involved an 8 hour operation to remove a blister cyst the size of a grapefruit. His surgeon told him that the vodka actually burned it onto his pancreas.

Church and beach tomorrow.

Ricky is snoring. It's 1:05am. Ricky looks like a sleeping baby, but snoring like hell.

I got to thinking about what the therapists say concerning family support through all of this and how much it means to recovery, and almost started crying, but not for myself, I certainly could use some more, but I hate to think of what I'm putting my family through from 1400 miles away. FUCK!!!!

Day 4

> "I suppose I've got a lot to atone for, but I'm not alone there, none of us are. We are all just human beings. So many emotions are darting through me right now. I wonder if it's Instant Karma in slow motion? He, who is without sin, cast the first stone. Right?"

Went down to the tables to have a smoke just before dawn. Rocky the squirrel shows up around 7 am and jumps up on the table looking for food. She's really cool, but nobody has any food, so you could tell she got kinda' pissed.

So Jim went up to his room and brought her down some peanut butter crackers. When she saw him walking back across the alley in his bright blue tank top stretched over his Santa Clause belly (only Jim has black hair) she got really excited and ran over to him to take a cracker out of his lumber jack hands. She sat there next to the tree and ate it, then jumped back on the table to say thank you, I guess, and then she ran through an opening in a wooden fence across the alley.

Gone. We'll see her tomorrow I hope.

The shit you experience in rehab. Amusing as hell. Probably better off not trying to analyze any of it. It is what it is. Besides, I've got enough on my mind right now. Don't we all.

Sensitive people. Cool. Interesting as all hell.

Salena comes down, straight A NYU student, strung out on dope, but so smooth and smart, jet black hair and cat green eyes. Always helping people. She lights up a smoke and says, "Fuck the pain box" (phone), and I said, "Yeah, I hear ya Salena."

10:20pm. Ricky comes into our apartment for help on a rehab writing assignment concerning his brandy addiction. Still can't understand a word he fuckin' says. Really a sweet little guy. Looks like a baby, I swear!

OK, I'm now back down at the tables.

Got to meet crazy Janet, who lives on a ranch in Wyoming. She sits and quilts through all the meetings. Then one day Janet opens up and says, she's 55 and hooked on booze and percs.

Her first husband died of a brain aneurism, and her new husband is a drunk who has almost died of pancreatitis. He was too fuckin' plastered to remember the pain, so he still pounds away. Janet wants to quit.

She was really cool on the beach today playing volleyball with everybody in the ocean (great beach). She cooks and cooks, but hardly eats anything. Had gastric by-pass surgery 2 years ago.

Her roommates love her of course. She's the motherly type.

Oh yeah, last night in a special meeting, a big guy who never talks, just sits and stares at the floor looking like Boris Karloff in the original Mummy movie. The light was just so, so that his eyes looked black and sunken. Scary.

I kept my eyes on him while Calvin from England told the dark story of his alcoholism. That was scary too.

I called Layla "Miss. St. Croix." She laughed and said she would follow me anywhere after that compliment! Plunked her blanket down right next to me on the beach. She's a little heavy and just a bit self conscious about it. Pretty face. She talked about how great Cavalry Chapel church was earlier in the day, which it was.

Did I tell you I got saved?

Walked right down front, the first person in front of 3700 people. Before it was over, there were over a hundred souls behind me. Randolph and Mark among them.

Fabulous feeling.

I'd done it once before at my brother Kevin's church in York, PA., but I got lost somewhere between then and now. This disease is a tricky bastard.

Jimmy, from the "Dirty J" (his nickname for New Jersey) shared at a meeting that he stole his dad's car at the ripe old age of 13. Started shootin' the dragon at 15. Heroin is hell.

He was such a monster on the football field that his coach would give him oxy's before and after every game (way to go coachy boy). Jimmy would hide a couple oxy's and trade them for needle juice out on the streets.

His dad found him OD'd and blue in his bedroom twice, damn near dead. Brought him back both times, thank God.

Jimmy loves the Phillies and the Eagles, so he can't be all bad. Jimmy was a two time All State first team linebacker in high school. Tough as granite.

Get this. Alice comes down to the tables and announces that she wants to be called "Fuckin' A" from now on, and pulls down her bottom lip to show us 2 star tattoos.

I said, "Shit Fuckin' A", that must've hurt." She said, "Hell no, I smoked some crack then rode the dragon. Didn't feel a damn thing."

There was almost a brawl in the big meeting tonight. Would have gotten bloody, believe me. Glad the techs jumped in and stopped it. A nice little fist fight would've been fun though!

Ricky keeps asking me how to spell words. Shit, I thought, he was in education. Oh well.

I also had to explain some stuff about vitamins and natural herbs to Dr. Sorrentino today. Hell, I feel like a teacher and a doctor sometimes. Dr. Garbage Head. Funny. No?

Oh yeah, Miss St. Croix sat next to me at the meeting that almost saw the brawl, and told me that she had isolated all day and was very depressed. Said she'd like to come down to the tables, but she's allergic to smoke. She's thinkin' about getting an "epi" pen so she can stick herself in the leg with it every 5 minutes so she could smoke and bullshit too.

She's a travel writer and real estate landlord. She hasn't been able to write for months though. Doesn't know if she wants to go back to the island. Too many skeletons and crooked politicians. Besides, her husband is down there.

I saw her writing in a notebook after the meeting. She looked up and smiled. I smiled back and gave her a thumbs up. She's hiding something painful and I can see it and feel it.

I've only got 2 Black and Mild cigars left. Tomorrow I'm gonna get tobacco and papers and start rolling my own smokes. Enrico had some Indian cigarettes that his brother had sent him from the war in Iraq.

Jessie piped up and said her cousin was the youngest sergeant in the history of the US Army.

Like I said. Rehab.

Almost forgot, talkin' to Butchie at the tables this afternoon. He's had 9 or 10 angioplasties and 1 bypass surgery. Was on the North Miami police force for 24 years. His demons are percs, zannys and booze. Butchie hates fuckin' cops now. What's that all about?

A girl from Texas had a headache today, so Butchie pressed his thumbs into her forehead and then squeezed the skin between her thumbs and index fingers. She almost passed out, but her headache was gone.

Then he lit a cigar and said that he was still a little worried about his heart, and that his two boys were more worried about his life and death battle with his demons. He's gonna win, bet your badge on it.

I said, "Butchie, I hope you don't fuckin' die on me today, buddy."

Just talkin' to Joelle at midnight smoke break down at the tables and she told me about the new girl, Margaret, who didn't get off on two 80mg oxy's (strange), so she went back to booze. Very kind girl, Joelle, and good friend.

Anyway, Joelle is 26 and looks 16. Booze, roxies, zannys, and pot chased her to south Florida. She was the head of a high school child study team up north. Her boss is also an addict and will hold her job for her, but she really doesn't want to leave Florida now.

Hear that a lot.

Good night.

Shit, a tech just told me that I can't roll my own cigarettes because it might be a trigger for a pothead. I said, "Hell, I was a pothead too."

Day 5

"When I look back over my life, I can see where I made a lot of good choices and a lot of bad ones, too. The bad ones are winning right now. But I've got faith in the future. At this moment in time, I really have no other choice. I just keep wondering what challenges, mysteries and obstacles might lie ahead. Little scared. Little exited."

7:10 am. Down at the tables for a smoke and coffee.

Butchie stood up and this awesome giant rainbow curled around behind his head.

Dr. Sorrentino just walked by. He's a real nice guy. Think he might study up on vitamins and herbs.

Wayne's new roommates are absolute pigs and he is really pissed off. Gangsta rap twenty-four, seven.

Wayne went to school to be a commercial airline pilot, but eventually got shot down because of his eyesight. However, he did get a private helicopter pilot license and had a little business giving people rides. His eyesight got worse and he had to switch careers and sold medical supplies for a while. Now he waiter's in a restaurant.

Slippery slope.

He saw a lot of destruction and death on the streets while living in Chicago during his booze and crack head period. Now it's just booze. And a lot of it. The booze hides the memories, but it is destroying and killing him. He can't take it anymore, 46 years old.

Starts raining like hell and everybody steps out from the canopy covering the tables and dances around with their mouths open and arms out.

Like something right out of *One Flew Over The Cuckoo's Nest.* I just watched.

Seems like everyone's hands are shaking this morning, probably post acute withdrawal syndrome (PAWS). Devil slowly moving out and God moving in?

Salena (remember her?) is from Latvia, brilliant girl, moved here when she very young. When she was 8 years old a guy tried to grab her out of an elevator in the apartment house she lived in. She got away, he had a blade against her neck and she ran like hell when the elevator door opened before he thought it would.

A day later people were smelling this horrible stench, come to find out it was a dead little girl in the same guy's apartment who had tried to grab Salena. Her best friend. That's when she started sticking bobby pins into light sockets, pulling her hair out and doing other self destructive things. Raped at 14, she got pregnant but had a miscarriage.

Talking to Albert, a really cool gay guy. TV news reporter for ABC Hartford, CT and ABC Miami. Lost his job when viewers thought he looked high. Booting meth will do that, you know. Relapsed once but says he's gonna make it this time, and go for a job in the Philly market.

Jay, 24, the EMT from North Carolina, likes oxy's and saving lives. One of the things that haunt him is thinking and having nightmares about a scene where he walked into a house with 4 people shot dead. A mother, her sixteen and eighteen year old sons, as well as their 3 year old little brother who was shot in the back of the head still holding his spoon and sitting at the kitchen table. Poor little guy never even got a chance to finish his Captain Crunch. Every time Jay sees the little guy in his mind's eye, two oxy blues help take the memory away. A drug friend of the father committed the murders. He was caught in Utah. Daddy is now in the slammer for drugs.

Jay's oxy supplier and her mother recently blew up and were killed in a meth lab explosion. Been a lot on Jay's mind lately.

Getting and staying clean is no easy thing.

Brianna came running into the med room so happy that she's been clean for 42 days. Says how lucky she is about surviving the night she OD'd 3 times and flat lined. Her friends gave her CPR and mouth to mouth even though she was throwing up blood all over. Got her to the hospital, finally admitted to the ICU. A couple days later her friends came up and brought her some heroin and a needle. She booted it up and promptly died again, but the doctors brought her back. She's had enough of that she says.

Just got back from midnight smoke where "Fuckin' A" is working on her goodbye to drugs letter.

Oh, Brianna OD'd four days after leaving the half-way house she'd been living in from a combination of booze, zannys and coke. God rest her tortured soul. The last thing she said to me is that she loved me like the big brother she never had. Sucks! Really sucks!

Day 6

"So many people here, from such varied backgrounds and ways of life. We may have arrived on different ships, but we're all in the same boat now. Sail or sink."

7:05 am. Down to the tables for coffee and a smoke.

Jon walks down and discovers an egg in his pocket, shows it to us and says, "I Don't know how it got there." Takes it over to the fence across the alley, cracks it a little and leaves it for Miss Rocky. Never knew squirrels liked raw chicken eggs.

Doyle tells us that he screwed his best friend's mom a few years back and it still bothers him.

Found out that last night a guy we called Typo had a seizure and the ambulance took him off into the darkness. Good luck, Typo.

Karen locked herself in her bathroom last night hysterical, the techs busted in and got her quick so she didn't have time to cut herself up too much. Karen likes mutilating herself and huffing inhalants.

Salena finished her story today in group. Told how she went to high school graduation all dressed up in Gothic, shaved the back of her head and had her friend draw a big Smiley Face on it with a magic marker. Left home and went on a 2 year booze and coke dealin' run that summer. She hung herself but somebody found her in time and cut her down. Got clean and went to a small, but extremely well respected college, (very high IQ), 3.96 GPA and tutored in all subjects and multiple languages, then went to NYU about the time her best friend forever, Liz, hung herself to death.

Salena went on another run over that one. Spent her 25th birthday in the Clarion City jail in sunny Florida. Her parents finally caught up with her on a pigmy goat and chicken farm in Indiana. Back in Florida again she took 32 hits of acid, slit her wrists and jumped into a lake with the alligators.

When she was 29 she weighed 98, no, 85 pounds. And got her meals at the dollar store. Lived in a real filthy trailer park. Got knocked up then found the father of her fetus hanging dead in the next room. She kicked and punched him after she cut him down, but like the song says, "Baby It Was Too Late." Wound up with a 10 bag a day heroin habit. Finally ended up here in rehab. She left today for a halfway house.

We are all gonna miss her. Very special person. Good wishes, girl!

April's therapist has been pissing her off and upsetting her because April keeps talking about her twin baby boy, Jamison, who died at 3 months old. And her therapist keeps saying, "Get over it." We talked about it at church. She says the surviving twin, Dustin, talks a lot to his dead brother. I believe it.

Singer Raymond left today for his Baltimore home. Gonna miss him and his voice, too. Oh yeah, Salena miscarried for the second time.

Day 7

"I had a dream early this morning that my wife Susan floated into my room with a light blue sweater on. Her pretty face smiling and wanting me to come home. I was so happy! But it never came true. I woke up and almost cried. The gut-punching sting of reality. "

Made my way down to the tables about 7 am for coffee and a smoke, trying to shake off my dream.

Chatted with Ike from Connecticut, who talks a lot about turbine engines (boring as hell). It's his 25th wedding anniversary today. At the AA meeting last night at church, the speaker named Eric, impressed Ike and Ike asked him to be his AA sponsor.

The name Eric still makes him smile, but upsets him at the same time. It reminds him of the night Eric, Ike's best friend, hid under a car during a barroom brawl of some sailors on leave. One of them saw Eric, reached down under the car and shot him in the head. Eric was 17 years old, and that was 35 years ago.

Shit like that never goes away.

Happy anniversary Ike. Getting wasted everyday dulls the sharp memory of that night. Ike is ready to face life on life's terms now, or so he says. The other day he was out in the street stopping cars and telling the drivers he was Jesus Christ. I know how he feels about trying to forget certain things. I think everybody here does. But Ike's out there, man. Pretty fucked up dude if you ask me.

My muscles hurt from trying to lift weights again yesterday at LA Fitness. When will I ever learn that my broken back just can't do that anymore?

Paulie, from Texas, sits down and lights a long dark cigarette shipped to him from back home in Texas. Says he doesn't feel good and it must be the crud. I'm thinking, "What the hell is the crud?", but just say, "Hey dude, I hope you get to feeling better." He says no matter what he won't miss primary group, and doesn't.

Crystal, a big blonde in her 30's, who is a drug counselor at a federal prison in Indiana, would slip out and smoke crack in her car between sessions. Inmates called her out on it. Busted! Nobody else, including her boss, picked up on it till the prisoners ratted her out.

Can't fool an addict.

Dylan's chair just collapsed in meeting, funny as hell. I helped him up.

Right then Albert, the gay TV reporter, was telling us how he smoked cracked with a famous Governor's daughter at a private school near Miami, and how his boyfriend doctor would shoot him up with meth, and helped him piss away $46,000 on dope in just the past year alone. Decided he better get his ass into rehab, and save his life.

Saw Dr. Sorrentino again today. So far, so good on my blood work.

Julie, my primary group therapist, just told us about a girl who smoked a joint laced with PCP. It fucked her up so bad that it was called progress when she took a shower. With her clothes on.

Somewhere at another rehab in south Florida. Shot out. Damn shame. Gone forever.

Brian's cracking his neck.

Paulie stares out over the top of his inhaler.

Jim, Rocky's buddy, is gonna sell his house in PA and move down here. Drinking (a quart of vodka a day) at home is too much of a reminder for him to tolerate and even have a prayer of staying sober. Jim's got guts and good instincts.

Brian, as Julie stepped out, just told me that he saw one of us steal a candy bar from the church last night, and doesn't know if he should snitch or not. I say, "Hey Bri, do what you think is best." Our little group is very close and quite interesting.

Gave my wife Susan full power of attorney today over all my affairs. I trust her completely, that's one fine woman, man do I miss her. My hero.

Rocky showed up this afternoon at the tables, and Jim fed her a cracker.

New guy, Randall from Oklahoma, who is addicted to sex and crack cocaine, got saved last night at Calvary chapel.

Another day in paradise.

Day 8

"Another dream last night. This time about my dog CoCo. My brother, Dr. Kevin Trout, a Pastor, gave her to me for handling our Mother's funeral. I've had so many good dogs in my life. This is the first time I've ever had to leave one behind. Hurts. Well, back at it. Life, that is. Love you, CoCo."

Yepper, down at the tables at sunrise sharp for coffee and smokes. Got one more Black & Mild till this afternoon when they take all 80 of us to Publix to shop. We get $60 a week each to spend on groceries. The store nervously gears up for this weekly adventure. Have to buy my own smokes, though. We all do.

No Rocky the squirrel yet this morning, because Shadow the community cat is buttering everybody up at the tables looking for head scratches and free food.

Rocky, she's watching from across the alley near the trees by the wooden fence.

They finally let Wayne move. He's my new roommate now. He takes a drag off his Marlboro light and says, before all the smoke is gone from his lungs, that he sometimes drank a gallon of white wine in the first two hours he was awake in the morning.

A new guy named Sean, from Wisconsin, says he's got a buddy coming in from Wisconsin tomorrow. His name is Wally and all he talks about is killing people. He's had eleven operations to remove shrapnel, from his time in Vietnam, and has been haunted and broken down by the defoliant Agent Orange that got into his lungs and took a piss all over his other organs. Brain included. Hard core vodka man.

After Wally and I got to know each other, he showed me a letter that he wrote to the dead Vietnamese family of 6 that he murdered in a small village in Vietnam. Vietnam wasn't very nice to Wally, and Wally wasn't very nice to Vietnam. On one of the several occasions when Wally was pronounced dead, he had a near-death experience, in which he saw some old friends, relatives, and Jesus. Thanks for serving soldier.

Mark, one of my first roommates is leaving this morning. What a fuckin' fantastic young man. Not only did he kick the shit out of the dragon, but he is an ass kickin' piano player, too. Mark is a little apprehensive about going home, but that's a good thing. Keeps a man on guard. Really gonna miss him. Love ya bro, and thanks for the stamps and envelopes.

I asked Ricky for a smoke to hold me over, and like a fuckin' magician, he pulled out 5 Newports. Through my first exhale, I gaze up and see a beautiful rainbow dip down across the morning sky, between Wally and "Fuckin' A". .

Both cool ass people battling the disease of addiction. Wally says the Viet Cong were easier to fight. Wow!

Brian, (in my primary group) has a nasty ass spider bite on his leg and one on the crack of his ass. He shows a couple of u guys, who didn't really want to see them. Getting worse day by day. Could get serious, looks real bad on that leg. I didn't have the opportunity to see the one on his ass. Gratitude, oh yeah!

Layla, aka Miss St. Croix, admits in morning big-group that she has a food addiction in addition to her drinking problem. Now there's honesty for you.

Lots of iguana running around, some of those bastards are almost as long as one of the tables! Glad they're vegetarians.

Talking to Thad from Ohio, who wanted to share his near death experience. One night, near Columbus, Ohio he ate four valium wagon wheels, and shoved a needle full of the dragon into his nice plump neck vein.

Next thing he knew, or should I say didn't know, was that he was dead in the front passenger's seat of a car. The driver wanted to dump him out on a back street, but a female friend of Thad's who was in the back seat punched and punched at the driver and persuaded him to take Thad to a hospital, where they had to defib him on the backs of his legs, because they feared a chest shock might blow up his overworked heart.

They pumped out his stomach with charcoal. He came back to life and started ripping tubes and hoses out of his body, so they shot him up to put him back down.

Thad also admitted in big-group to having sex with a man while he was in prison. A very hard thing for him to do.

Oh yeah, Brianna, Fuckin' A and Nikki say they are gonna be in the "Girls in Recovery" calendar. Everybody thought it would be a cool idea to have a calendar like that.

Never happened though, of course.

Day 9

> *"It's so cool to see all of these addicts totally straight*
> *for the first time in like, forever. Their personalities seem*
> *to take on new and bright colors and they shine. Me too*
> *I suppose. Or so I've been told."*

Tables. What else, right?

In morning big-group, Philip, the top clinician was real pissed and told everybody that we had a thief among us. Stole rings and money from Crazy Janet and a bunch of other stuff from a few rooms. Philip asked the stealing shitbag to own up, and he would work with him, or her. The thief stayed quiet. I just found out that they caught the little prick. Gone, with charges pressed. Justice be done. Hang 'em high.

In primary group Dylan said, "If I Don't say goodbye, you never have to leave." Pretty good line, I told him I'd use it in a song.

Ray Cummings, the CEO/owner of the place, held a meeting during big-group about "resentments."

Here's how it worked; As we went around the room, for each of our resentments, we tossed a square of toilet paper into a plastic trash can. You could hear a pin drop. Then Mr. Cummings took the trash can out into the parking lot, and set the paper inside on fire. It burned like hell in the hot Florida sun, as we all stood around and watched it and cursed it.

We finally, as they say, saw the light. It was great, a very intense ritual.

Played guitar around the pool tonight. Had a ball. I'm gonna ask my wife Susan to send the Bentley (my guitar) down. Felt good to sing and play. I used crazy Janet's guitar. She doesn't play though.

Julie, my therapist, prayed for me today. Julie is, well, special.

Heading down to the tables for a midnight smoke.

Day 10

*"One thing for sure. I could be in a lot worse places.
Fuck, I'm in South Florida, where the sun always shines
and the water is always warm. Everybody's gotta be
somewhere! And if I can't be home, what the hell. Plus
Julie's here. A true Angel from Heaven. She has helped
me so much."*

Fed Rocky a bagel this morning. She was very grateful, and cute
as all hell. She couldn't eat it all, so the birds cleaned up what she
left behind.

Now, I just spoke with Jeanie, a young blonde girl from New
Hampshire, and her stories were so moving, scary and upsetting,
that I feel I must dedicate this whole night's writing to what she
revealed.

I really don't know where to start, so here goes.

Okay, Jeanie is a smallish girl with beautiful eyes and an aura
about her that I have never before experienced. As her blonde
hair swirled around on the warm Florida evening breeze, she
started by telling me how she king pinned a huge pot distribution
business in Boston, where she attended a Christian college.

She not only supplied the college students, but also the brutal
gang syndicate known as the New England Kings. Not only were
they her grateful customers, but they had her back, if you know
what I mean. She was like their fair haired little Goddess. They

loved and protected her as if these notorious ass kickers were transformed into soft little puppy dogs and kittens. Subtle power, that's Jeanie.

But, the part of our conversation that got me shivering was the part about the woman who crab-walked belly up out of her parents master bathroom across the floor and up onto her parents bed as Jeanie lay there alone watching TV, with the lights on and her parents and sisters out.

She was the only one at home. She was frozen with fear as the tallish woman with short red hair slithered up and across the foot of the bed nearly touching Jeanie's feet. She stared in shock as the woman crawled off the other side of the bed and crab-walked out the other door into the hallway. Disappearing.

No doubt, Jeanie was as close to being as scared to death as a child could possibly be. She was ten years old and it was the first time her parents had ever left her home alone.

About ten minutes later she was shaken back from that demon world by the sound of her parents and sisters coming in through the front door. She ran in a breathless panic out the bedroom door and headed down the stairs when she felt, 'a foot or something', trip her up halfway down the stairs.

Resilient and flexible as any ten year old she made it to her mother, physically unhurt, and told her about the crab woman. Her mother turned ghost white, her jaw dropped and her eyes flew open wide.

Jeanie's mom, trembling, screamed out, "Jeanie, tell your father – tell your father!"

At first she said "No." Something inside her was trying to tell her not to. But she did, and he too, turned sheet white. Cold sweats. Fear, sadness, and powerlessness gripped him around his throat choking and choking him.

That was the prelude to Jeanie hearing the story behind it all; When Jeanie's father was an infant, on the same piece of land on which he later built the home they now live in, as he lay on the grass one day, a tallish woman with short red hair was hanging up clothes on the clothesline next door, when a man ran up behind her and stabbed her six times in the back, killing both her and her unborn child.

Writhing on her back, almost in a crabwalk, the last thing the woman saw before everything went black, was the upside down vision of Jeanie's infant father. Jeanie's family thinks that the crabwoman's spirit somehow entered her dad's body that day as he lay on the grass, and perhaps she could not bear the thought of her fetus dying with her.

So, instead of traveling to heaven or hell, her spirit moved into Jeanie's dad and cannot or will not move on.

Only a theory. They've had many through the years.

Jeanie's mom and her two sisters have all had many encounters with the crabwoman. The only one in the family who has not is her dad. FUCKIN' WEIRD, huh?

Day 11

"The more I talk to these people, clients and staff alike, and get to know how amazing they are, the more awed I am. It's like unearthing a treasure one day at a time."

Tables – church – beach.

We played football in the ocean . I was quarterback because all I had to do was stand still and pass the ball. Still killed my back though and I had to drop out of the game. The rules were we weren't allowed to play in less than waist deep water, because that would've been too easy.

I found a perfect little shell and a piece of coral. Want to give them to my wife, but I don't know if she'll want them. I have no idea how she's feeling about us. She's in south Jersey, I'm in south Florida. Time will tell. It's really all up to God at this point. I love her and miss her. Hurts like hell.

Oh yes, yes, yes the water temperature was at least 85°. Nice man, nice. Our team lost.

This morning Rocky came half way down the closest tree to the tables and stared at us. We fed her. She loves us, and we love her. Found some peanuts in the cabinet that either Mark or Patrick left behind. They are Rocky's now.

Day 12

*"Trying to figure out whether I can do all of this or not.
It's really strange to come from living in my own home
with my family for over 30 years to being thrown in to a
commune of recovering addicts. Like day and night.
Should I just hop on a plane and go home? I'd so love to.
But I can't do that to Susan. Not now. And I shouldn't do
it to myself either. Gonna try and stick it out. God give
me strength?"*

Tables. You guessed it. Let's face it, us addicts love to drink coffee and smoke cigarettes.

Hell of a way to spend my son's birthday, huh? Sucks!!!!!!!!!!!!!!!!

What a terrific young man, I'm so proud of him I could cry. Gonna have to do for this year, though. He knows I love him.

Patty, a basketball star out of Trenton, NJ shared her story in big-group this morning. Like a lot of us she was a garbage head. Booze, pot, oxys, zannys and ecstasy. Pretty sure booze was her major demon, and the rest went hand in hand. Beautiful person inside and out.

When she went to Mercer State College in southern NJ to play basketball, her drinking and zannys especially (tricky combo) kicked into high gear. Now here she is.

She was born on June, 19th, the same birthday as mine. Small and interesting world, isn't it?

By the way, one of the few things I never tried was Ecstasy. Wow, how did I miss that one!

I got talkin' to my roommate Wayne today, who now lives in Naples, Florida. Yep, him and his girlfriend, Tessie. Wayne is a very classy guy whom I thought was merely an alcoholic. Turns out (as I mentioned briefly earlier) he was also a crackhead in West Chicago for 10 years.

Pistols pointed at his head 5 times, one rifle and a couple knives, too. He was kidnapped at gunpoint in his own Cadillac. Man, he's lucky to be alive.

His father was vice president of one of those large companies that manufacture coffee-makers. So Wayne didn't like it when I re-poured coffee back through the coffee maker. A trick I learned from my Mother-in-law. Genius, no doubt.

Gonna miss Wayne, one damn good roommate.

Heading down to the tables for a midnight smoke.

Thad, fresh out of an Ohio prison and a thug named Tom, just down from the badlands of Philadelphia almost got into a fight because Tom was spreading a rumor that Thad was fuckin' one of the girls.

Not true, Thad is married and was really pissed because coupling (as they call it), is grounds for being kicked-out of rehab on the spot.

Speaking of the badlands of Philly, it reminds me of one of my New Jersey therapists' best girlfriends, from a wealthy family, who went down there to cop dope one too many times. She was kidnapped, raped and murdered and left in the darkest part of an old and dangerous parking lot. The bastards covered her body with peanut butter so the rats would eat her (the evidence) quicker. They filled her mouth and vagina with peanut butter too.

Thad reported Tom's rumor to his primary therapist. Smart move. Anyway, Thad could kick his cocky ass, as many of us would like to have seen. I'd like to bust his face myself! Tom sucks.

Yesterday in big-group, Willson, a tall thin black kid, with tightly pulled back jet black hair, admitted that he had shot and killed four people in Saint Thomas while dealing pot. Laughing the whole time, showing no remorse at all. A lot of people in group were really fuckin' upset. The dude got away with murder, so far anyway.

Just wrote a fairly simple vitamin regimen up for big Rave, also from St. Thomas. Looks like a 6'6" scary Ray Charles. He always wears black sun-glasses because he is blind in one eye and his bad eye looks strange and scary.

I learned how to play dominos today with some of the guys from the Caribbean. Never knew dominos was actually a game. I just thought they were something that you set up and then knocked down.

Can't stop thinking about my daughter Dana. I spent her birthday this year at the South Jersey rehab.

Man, I've got to get a handle on this disease! Startin' to.

Day 13

> "We have all been calling the phone, the pain box.
> Because that's what it is. Taking turns using cell phones
> for fifteen minutes a night really sucks. Let me tell you, I
> see more tears than smiles at those sessions. Most of us
> just give up on that pain box. People on the other end
> just don't understand. Not their fault. They really have
> no clue as to what we are going through."

In primary group today, Julie had me read the poem I wrote yesterday. Not bad for a 2 minute exercise in rhyme and perhaps a seasoning of reason. Gonna make a copy of it tonight and give to her tomorrow.

Jon's back. Remember, he's Steve's brother. The dead one that looked like me. Still says I look exactly like him. He died this past April, as you know. Strangely flattering in some sort of perverse way.

Keep in mind now that I am an addict and alcoholic totally straight now for the first time in ages. Very tuned into all kinds of weird shit. Still haven't seen a UFO though, but Jeanie's parent's have.

Speaking of Jeanie again, the monk story, Wow-D-Dow! Get this. Jeanie's mom had a young friend, a gay fellow, who became a monk. Well, the poor guy died young and was cremated. As

Jeanie and her mom sat in her kitchen, there was a ceremony in their backyard where his ashes were spread in the grass. Jeanie and her mom could see the ceremony through the window in the kitchen door. As his ashes hit the ground, Jeanie and her mom heard what sounded like a low hum. It grew louder and louder and louder until it shook the walls of the house and filled their ears, hearts and their souls. It was what they both described as a thunderous mantra. It sounded as if thousands of monks were chanting and lifting the gay monk's soul into heaven.

Then it stopped, as suddenly as it had begun. Moments in time that Jeanie and her mother cannot explain, yet will never forget. They were overcome by emotion and could not stop holding each other and crying.

Amazing.

Day 14

"At times there is a part of me that really likes this situation. If it hadn't been for missing my family, of course. I haven't really had time to dwell on the future. You are taught here how to live in the NOW, how to try and just do the next right thing. To let go and let God, and to forgive."

Petted Shadow this morning down at the tables. Pettin' with one hand, and smokin' a Black and Mild cigar in the other.

My 30th day without pot, booze, percs or zannys. Never thought that would happen. God does work in mysterious ways, especially in south Florida it seems.

Ricky just came up to our apartment (which everyone started calling The Penthouse because we had carpet instead of tile on the floors) he was sick as a dog. I made him some mint tea and he went to sleep.

Wayne is in the bathroom gagging like hell, as he does every time he brushes his teeth.

Some new guy was feeling me out down at the tables. We think he's the one who stole Rave's CD player. I'd really love to kick his fuckin' ass! Might as well cut Rave's heart out with a chainsaw than to steal his music.

Thad, Doyle and some others have been borrowing coffee from us. Hope Wayne doesn't get pissed off, because we're almost out.

One of the techs took Ricky to see the nurse around 7am.

"Fuckin' A" has to go to the dentist today. Her transformation has been no less than miraculous. She looks good, feels good and "really has it goin' on, buddy." As "Fuckin A" herself would say.

Fifty-nine year old Clem told us his hard core alcoholic story in big- group today. I'll never forget one thing he said, "First a man takes a drink, then the drink takes a drink, then the drink takes the man."

You got it Clem.

Patty just told us in primary that she killed a 10" centipede on the 1st floor last night. and she's petrified. Looking out through the palm trees, I just saw a flock of green parrots. So tropical looking.

There's a rumor that Burt Reynolds is here somewhere, and Jeanie, bless her young soul, doesn't know who he is. If he is here I haven't seen him yet.

We were role playing in primary today with Julie. She had Paulie from Texas, the guy with the "crud" and inhaler, talk to his dead father (played brilliantly by Wayne). It was so intense. Paulie was crying and saying he was so sorry for beating his dad up, and for pulling the plug in the hospital so his dad would die. Very heavy session.

Julie got a quiet girl in our group named Cindy to share how she took a friend to a concert, got him drugs, and how he overdosed on them and died. Cindy is a very lovely girl who just happens to like shooting dope.

We all have issues here. And talking about them out in the open helps. Thank God for Julie!

She even got me to tell about the total stranger who committed suicide, perhaps because of me. First time I ever said it out loud to any living soul. Let alone to the 8 in our group.

Church at Calvary Chapel was awesome as usual. On the way back in the van, EMT Jay from North Carolina, told us about a garbage head evil motherfucker who tied his girlfriend up down in a basement and burned her feet off! They later found her crawling down the sidewalk. One tough bitch.

Karen told us how she and some friends took care of a crackhead son of a bitch who had threatened to kill her. They took the guy out in the woods, tied him to a tree with rope and duct tape. After she sliced him up and down with a razor blade, they threw bags of salt all over him. This torture went on for 4 days. On the fifth day they cut him down like a sack of horseshit and he just disappeared. Coyotes maybe? Who knows? Just GONE.

Fun church bus talk, huh? Hey, we've all been through more shit than most people can imagine. Just sitting here in the van all dressed up for church we had a bond. We shared some of our stories. What the hell.

Allen from St. Thomas, and Cherl from New York both got saved tonight at the altar. Everybody clapped, cried and cheered.

Wayne said he heard Cindy was pissed off. Something about Randolph.

Anyway, Shadow started our day at the tables and ended it there too. Cool ass little rehab cat.

Oh yeah, Randolph (the fire-bug) started a fire today in a trashcan out by the tables. We all covered for him. Maybe that's why Cindy is pissed.

Day 15

"I think I'm the only person, at least one of the very few down here who hasn't gotten a letter or card since I've been here. I'm really ashamed to admit that fact. It hurt for a while but not anymore. Just gotta suck it up and be strong. Why not, what else can I do?"

Didn't make it down to the tables early this morning. Missed my girl Rocky. Had just enough time for coffee and a smoke before the 9 am big-group meeting.

Sat up front so I could hear Dylan tell his story. Poor fucker, 22 years old with a huge self carved cross on the top of his left wrist. Must be 8" high and 4" across. Ugly as hell and even hurts to look at. Dylan gouged it out with a knife and razor blade during a drug and alcohol induced blackout. That thing ain't never goin' away. Hopefully it will act as a brutal reminder to stay straight. Hope so.

Dylan's parents put him on Ritalin when he was just 4 years old. Up until he was 13 or 14, every time he did something, anything wrong, his dad would whip him bare assed 25 times. 25 lashes. He would actually take Dylan to the store to pick out the belts. Still has scars. Another creative form of punishment from good ol' daddy boy, was pouring dangerously hot, hot sauce down the little guy's throat. Here again, he also made little Dylan go with him to buy the liquid fire, and actually had to sign a waiver absolving the store of any responsibility should Dylan die, become brain dead or go insane.

Took him at least three days to recover after each dose of punishment. Sometimes longer. And they wonder why Dylan smokes pot, drinks the hard stuff and takes handfuls of pills to escape those childhood memories.

Thanks pop, love Dylan.

He comes up to penthouse 33 a lot. I made him a cheeseburger last night and sang and played *Let It Be,* by The Beatles for him, because if I didn't he threatened to do a header off my 3rd floor balcony.

Day 16

"Private sessions with my therapist, Julie are so cool. I really look forward to those. Very productive when it comes to understanding myself and what it takes to get myself back. Seems like she even knows what I'm thinking at times. Like she's known me all my life."

Got down to the tables early this morning to some wild ass conversations. Things like who's been stabbed the most or who will probably stay straight and who won't, etc., etc.. After that we went into the big room and I sat in the front row again, real close to Zeke who was going to tell his life story.

Zeke is a big guy, about 6'1", 225 lbs. and is 39 years old. He was born to 15 year old parents, and was then adopted by a Montana rancher and his wife. Zeke's new dad was a super duper macho guy. He was a big game hunter who traveled the world with his guns. In one big room of the house hung over $1 million of stuffed and mounted game that had fallen prey to Mr. Montana and his arsenal.

Gee, is there an animal heaven? Hope so.

He never told Zeke that he loved him, and he never took him hunting. So when Zeke started playing with Barbie dolls and dressing up like a cheerleader (and even wearing a wig), it wasn't long before dad freaked out in his mostly silent "manly" way and put Zeke on Ritalin and pretended he wasn't gay. At one point Zeke's dad found a gay magazine in his bedroom, and checked Zeke into the psych ward at the local hospital.

They would strip Zeke down and show him pictures of naked men doing fucked up things. An electric wire was attached to his penis and every time he got aroused by the pictures, you guessed it, they would shock him. It was a horrible thing to do and so painful that Zeke had to build a wall somewhere in his body between his brain and the pain, or he surely would've died or gone insane.

Zeke built that wall.

After that brilliant treatment had run its course, Zeke was still gay, of course. He was born gay and he's sure God wants him that way. To please his father, Zeke went out for the football team in high school and became an all-state center. He even got a scholarship to play at Montana State where he blew his knee out during his junior year.

After that Zeke bounced around the country tweaking (doing crystal meth) until he settled in Miami. Getting more and more fucked up on dope all the time. Oh yeah, he was addicted to food, as well as pot, meth, booze, and crack. Especially crack. A true garbage head, though.

He now has a house on the beach in Miami worth $2 million. If Zeke's dad were still alive, we can only assume that he would be proud seeing that Zeke is doing so well in recovery and business, but we all know how terribly wrong assumptions can be.

Today, Zeke's one hell of a man. His dad was an asshole. Period.

Day 17

"When you look around, whether inside or outside of rehab, it's not hard to find someone who is worse off than you are. Those are the people I love to talk to and try to help. Very important in my opinion."

Karen, a very pretty and smart 21 year old lesbian, who was very spiritual and colorful told some of her story today in big-group. She would have started with her childhood, but she has no memories until the age of 12. That's when her dad got very angry about his divorce to Karen's mom.

Karen didn't like Cliff, her mom's boyfriend, but she was still trying to be a good kid playing basketball as a release from her family problems and frustrations. One day when she got home from basketball practice a 15 year old boy named Lamar squeezed in the door of her house and ordered her to strip. Karen was just 14.

She was totally horrified and thought Lamar might kill her if she didn't take her clothes off. Lamar then raped her.

The next day in school he wrote all over the bathroom walls that he had fucked Karen and how it was all her idea. It was then that she got very depressed and suicidal. Since her parents were divorced, she didn't feel she could confide in either one of them. As Karen puts it, her mom and Cliff were "nut-jobs", and her dad lived too far away.

She became bulimic, and also became addicted to cutting herself. Not long after, she OD'd on inhalants and pills and was put on the list for a liver transplant. On top of all that her best friend Brittany died of melanoma at the tender age of 18. Life sucks sometimes. A lot of times. Damn! Karen's liver healed enough that she was taken off the transplant list. Her doctor said it was a miracle, but Karen said it was because of Brittany, her new guardian angel.

By this time Karen's head was all fucked up and again she OD'd on opiates, this time while babysitting. The parents found her on the bathroom floor when they got home. She survived only to be put into a psych ward where she was given electric shock treatments. She finally ran away from the hospital, and as her addiction to inhalants grew so did her self mutilation, which by this time also included burning herself.

Even after collapsing her lungs, she continued huffing 3-9 cans of inhalants a day, along with eating and snorting roxys and oxys. She was a garbage head like most of us here. Karen said she lived for the risk of dying. The last we heard she had cut herself so badly that she was taken to a hospital for emergency surgery, but nobody knows where. We are all praying for her.

Now it's midnight and time for one last cigarette down at the tables. Wally was there. He told me once again about all of his operations and near-death experience. But never mentioned Vietnam.

Good night. Pleasant dreams, buddy.

Day 18

"My mind is sharpening day by day, which allows me to more clearly reflect on just what the circumstances were that brought me down here. The answer is in the mirror. That guy just got wildly out of control. My fault. I'm not gonna blame it on my 'disease' anymore. I'm fighting it now. And winning."

Rocky's out this morning doing battle with the birds over the bagel and peanuts we put out for her. Shadow must be over by the pool or under the stairs in the shade.

Dylan came up to the penthouse again last night feeling suicidal and needing to hear *Let It Be* again. I'm thinkin', fuck man, choose another song will ya? But kept my mouth shut. Then we meditated and Dylan started to feel better.

The beach was great today, the water was 86 degrees and so clear we could see the fish swimming around our ankles. Everyone had a blast and hated to leave.

I played a few songs around the pool again tonight using my own guitar this time, which my wife had mailed down to me. Thanks babe. Clint played a new song he wrote about recovery.

You know, rehab is a brave new world for most of us, cruel and cool at the same time.

Great song Clint, "I'm impressed, man!" And I don't say that very often.

Day 19

"My music career is definitely taking a back-seat in my life for a change. It's about time. Everything needs a rest now and then. I'm already planning my next CD, though. I've got six new songs written for it already. But that project will have to wait a while. I've got more important things to do right at the moment. Like survive. One day at a time."

I was just talking to a new guy named Bingo. A heavyset black guy in his fifties, originally from Louisiana, but FEMA moved him to Oklahoma after hurricane Rita leveled his house. Bingo is a world class chef. He has cooked for the Rolling Stones, ZZ Top, Credence Clearwater Revival, Marilyn Manson, and others not so famous, but just as rich.

He was clean for 8 years after his daughter got her head blown off by her fiancée. But, seven months ago Bingo went on a crack run that landed him in the hospital with a coke induced cardiac arrest, where he was pronounced dead twice and finally zapped back to life. That was just a couple of months ago.

So last night in the med room Bingo has a heart attack right in front of me and was rushed to the hospital. I was trying to talk to him while he was lying on the floor, but he was out of it, and I thought he was dead. As far as we know he is still alive. That night during our midnight smoke we all said a prayer for him.

Another casualty of this relentless, conniving disease. Fuck you!

Day 20

> "Sometimes I wonder what I'm doing here and then Julie, my therapist, brings me back to earth and explains everything to me again. What am I going to do without her, this rehab, and these glistening people? Not to mention Bible Study with the 'Holy Mother' as we called our Bible Study teacher. Oh well, I was alone when I got here. I'll make it."

So much shit has happened the last couple of days that I feel totally overwhelmed and find it difficult to write tonight. I'm drained.

Fights, relapses, heart attacks, self mutilation, you name it.

But through all of that I see how awesome the people here are, both patients and staff. As I said "brave new world."

My therapists have all been awesome! Both here and in south Jersey.

Day 21

"I've made so many good friends in rehab that I feel
truly blessed. I guess wherever we are at any given time,
is where we are supposed to be. These people are
proving that. To me, anyway. We are like a team, and
nobody knows what we go through but us."

As usual, went down to the tables very early this morning. I thought I was alone, but then from the corner of my eye I saw "Fuckin' A" coming over out of the west walking across the alley in the morning darkness.

We sat down, lit up our smokes, and she told me, "Nelson, God must have put you in my life." I said, "Hey, 'Fuckin' A', the feeling is mutual." I have never witnessed a positive transition as vividly as I have in her. She detoxed up in south Jersey at the same place I did.

So far, so good. We are both still alive. Survivors.

We've only known each other for 38 days, yet it feels like a lifetime. It's like I'm her older brother and I'm looking out for her, same with little Jeannie.

I met "Fuckin' A"'s parents and Jeannie's mom and sister. I promised them all that I would look after their girls for as long as I could. And I intend to do just that. Jeannie told everybody yesterday that "Fuckin' A" was the most talented makeup artist she has ever seen, and believe me, for her age she's really been around.

Jeannie's immediate neighbors include Joan Rivers and Conan O'Brien. Jeannie says, "they're both really nice people."

Jeannie is talented as well. She played her violin at Carnegie Hall when she was just 12 years old.

I've realized that most addicts are very interesting and, for the most part, talented people. We have all lived at least two lives. Nobody else can ever know how our disease can kill and at the same time breathe a unique understanding of life into our souls. Especially, at the beginning of our transformations. We have all been through hell and back.

"Fuckin' A" is gonna cut my hair tonight after we get back from Publix and put our groceries away.

I heard that Willson, the killer from St. Thomas, got tossed out of here last night after he flipped out on a couple of the Techs. There seemed to be a glimmer of hope for him, hell, he went down to the altar at Calvary chapel church last Sunday and got saved. But the devil speaks loudly to Willson.

Ernesto, Ricky and my latest roommate just got out of bed. Little does the new guy know that he was screaming in his sleep for most of the night. I'm not gonna tell him.

It's 6:45 am and I'm gonna take a shower and go back down to the tables. I have a feeling it's gonna be another eye-opening day... What a ride!

"In the throes of addiction. Tried to keep it a secret.
I was trapped." – 2009

PART II: KILL SHOTS

Select stories I've been told by other addicts and alcoholics in the throes of early recovery - among the living, the dead must play their part.

Drunk In AC

Ted was a successful plumbing contractor from northern New York State. He loves beer. Loves it too much.

When he fell down the stairs and broke his nose (another of his many mishaps) during a BBQ at his home, he knew it was time to quit.

Again. Easier said than done.

Ted had been in rehab once before for alcohol. Soon after the broken nose mishap, he got pissed off at his wife about something he now can't recall, and decided to drive to Atlantic City, NJ. where he thought he could catch a plane to see some of his family in Ireland.

Ted loaded his truck with two 30-packs of beer, and off he went to Las Vegas East. He withdrew $10,000 for the "plane ticket" and a little for gambling from an ATM on the way.

Drunk before he was halfway to AC, and after learning there were no flights to Ireland from Atlantic City, Ted proceeded to spend a few hours at the poker tables and lost a quick $3,000, while drinking the whole time.

He had parked his truck in a nearby parking garage and spent four days and nights walking the streets, drinking and sleeping in his truck. Ted had lost one of his shoes on the first day, so here he was, stumbling around Atlantic City on one shoe with $7,000 bucks in his pocket.

He still has no idea how he got home, but he quickly checked himself back into a rehab, found God, and so far is doing pretty well.

Lucky man.

The Garage

Gary, 53, is an alcoholic and pillhead. But, he is also a hockey and wrestling coach, a good provider for his family, and a damn loving father and husband.

But Gary got so fucked up last week that he fell through the sliding glass door of the shower in his master bathroom.

When his wife got home, luckily just a few minutes later, Gary was unconscious and bleeding like a stuck pig.

Just one more episode in Gary's memory haunted life. He is always trying to blur the vision of finding his pop-pop hanging from a rafter in the garage when he was a teenager. A few years later, Gary was the first one to discover his father dangling from that same rafter.

Booze and pills were the only way Gary felt he could escape the horror of reliving those tormenting memories of the garage over and over again. A few days ago Gary checked himself into rehab fearing for his own life and sanity.

Gary turned out to be a good friend.

Before I left him I said, "Hey Gary, stay away from that fuckin' rafter."

He looked at me with a little crooked grin and said, "Just one minute at a time for now, right, Nel?"

I said, "Yeah man, keep in touch."

The Trouble With Brothers

Dale always liked to drink vodka, smoke a little weed, and pop an occasional oxy. It was kind of the norm where Dale grew up just outside of Detroit.

When Dale was 24, his younger brother clubbed his mother and older brother to death in their sleep with an axe handle and burned down the house to incinerate their bodies.

After that tragedy, Dale's drinking, smoking and pill popping took off like a rocket. Not long ago, Dale passed out in his car at a red light. His body literally could not absorb another drop of vodka and simply shut down.

An elderly couple found him and called 911 just in time to save his life. After a lengthy hospital stay, he's now here in rehab with the rest of us. It disturbs a lot of guys that he keeps on saying that he'd like to get all fucked up and blow his brother's brains out.

His good new buddy, Jeremy, keeps on telling him that it's not worth it. Jeremy left rehab before Dale and as they held each other crying, Dale wept "Why Jeremy, why?"

Jeremy grabbed him by the shoulders and said, "Hey bro, tell me and we'll both know."

Then I got Dale and me a cup of coffee and we lit a cigarette and just sat there in silence on the ground.

Dale was still crying a little. I looked up at a cloud.

Man, I'll tell ya, sometimes this world is one tough fuckin' place.

The Last Trip

Andrea said she felt really good at first, then the two hits of orange barrel acid (LSD) turned her into a petrified blob, while she watched her friend's faces melt like hot plastic.

She was so freaked that she tried to run through the sliding glass door that opened out onto a wooden deck. She hit the glass hard, breaking her nose, elbow, and splitting her forehead open (requiring 9 stitches).

One guy grabbed her and she bit a chunk out of his shoulder, then ran into the bathroom screaming. She looked in the mirror and saw a witch's face yelling at her, telling her she was dead and going to hell.

She smashed the mirror with a glass drinking cup and cut the palm of her hand, severing tendons and blood vessels. Two guys tried to hold her still but she was too hard to control, like she was super strong.

A big Spanish guy named Bull, who was himself just getting off on two hits of acid, punched Andrea real hard in the temple from behind. The punch knocked her out and they thought she was dead, so they wrote a note with her name on it and attached it to her left nipple with a stapler.

Her best friend JJ then drove her to the ER and when Andrea was pushed out of the car, JJ floored it and zoomed off.

Every time she tells her story, among friends or in therapy, she buries her face in her hands as she trembles and sobs. She still won't come clean as to what her deeper demons really are, but whatever happened to her must have been bad, real bad.

Andrea smokes Black & Milds and drinks about 2 gallons of coffee a day. No wonder she shakes.

Thank God for therapists like Julie and Miss Peggy Andrews, good therapists are lifelines for sure!

I've got to be honest here and admit that I can really relate to Andrea's freak out. While on acid during the summer of '71, I had a bad trip and nearly lost my mind. I won't go into details, but that experience is tied for 1st place as the worst day of my life.

Detoxing from booze, benzos and opiates is the other one. Anyway, I did a half a hit of orange barrel acid. It was a little orange pill shaped like a 55 gallon drum. After not feeling any effect after a half hour, I dropped the second half.

Big mistake!

After about 6 hours of pure hell, a buddy of mine, Tony Cetera, chased me down a handful of reds (secanol) which were supposed to bring me down. So I chewed them up, and they were capsules, and washed them down with a half pint of Seagram's 7.

It brought me down, too down, almost 6 feet down, if ya know what I mean. I lived through that disaster, but never dropped acid again.

I still get scared with an overwhelming sense of sadness and shame every time I think about that night. If it wasn't for the reds and the whiskey and Tony Cetera, I'm sure I would have tried to kill myself or lost my mind completely...If you want my advice, just stay away from acid, dangerous stuff.

I guess God has other plans for Andrea, and for me.

Man Overboard

Larry is a 60 year old criminal attorney who just can't seem to shake his daily cravings for straight rum and roxy's. He smokes pot and does mushrooms on occasion, too.

Larry was considered the best lawyer in his firm. After showing up in court one too many times loaded, his partners and his wife of 29 years refused to tolerate his behavior any longer. He was nearly out of a job and a marriage by the time he checked himself into rehab.

Larry could not step foot on his yacht without a drink in his hand and a roxy buzz in his head. His therapist encouraged him to sell the boat because it seemed to be a huge trigger for his addictions. He showed me a virtual tour of his boat. Fuckin' awesome! Must be nice to be rich. I only had about 40 days clean and sober at the time. Larry and I agreed that it would be much harder for him to abstain if he was to get on board that boat.

We met at rehab in south Florida and became good friends. We both like to fish. His yacht is for sale now, but he is looking for another.

He hopes he can stay sober.

But, during his active addiction he didn't see a problem with partying every day and night (drunk and high on roxys) even though his family and friends did.

Wow, can I relate to that!

He laughs about it now, but, while fucked up, Larry fell off his boat about a year ago and almost drowned. It shook his wife up so bad that she drank two rum and cokes (though she's not normally a drinker) and cried all the way back to their private dock. Larry doesn't remember it – he had blacked out.

It reminds me of a blackout I had once. I watched my neighbor's house burn down one night and didn't remember it the next day. A buddy, who was one of the responding firemen, told me about it the next morning. As soon as I realized how bad that blackout was I knew I had to cut back on my partying (but still wouldn't admit I had a real problem).

Recently, I got a phone call from Captain Larry. He said he wanted to take me shark fishing on his new boat – no booze or pills allowed!

I laughed and said, "You're on, buddy!"

18 Wheel Nightmare

Ronny was high when he threw a cantaloupe out the window of his best friend's car. Right on target, he hit a poor guy riding up the street on his bike right in the stomach. Ronny and his buddy laughed like hell until they saw the guy fall off his bike and get squashed by the 18-wheeler that was behind them.

They didn't stop and nobody saw the cantaloupe in flight, including the truck driver it seems. They read about the dead guy in the paper the next day.

Ronny can't get those images out of his head, so he gets wasted everyday to try and forget.

His friend, who was driving the car, put his dad's 9mm Glock in his mouth and pulled the trigger.

Ronny didn't have the guts to honor the suicide pact they had made so, in order to relieve himself of his demons, he self-medicated constantly by shooting heroin and meth, smoking crack and drinking.

Anything to kill the memories of that poor guy going under the truck, and his friend's suicide.

Now he's in rehab, but he ain't gonna make it.

I can feel it in my gut. He's a goner.

A Father's Nightmare

Adolph looked like hell when he showed up at rehab. He appeared like a rag doll with really sad eyes. I stuck my hand out at the butt-hut, and as he shook it I could feel his weakness and desperation. Adolph was a maintenance mechanic on the boardwalk in Seaside, New Jersey, where he worked on roller coasters, ferris wheels and other amusement rides.

He started drinking real heavy, even while working. His boss gave him a choice, go to rehab or hit the bricks.

Ralph's 16 year old son and two of his buddies robbed a gun shop one night, getting away with fourteen guns. Later that night in his son's bedroom, while the boys were mesmerized with a PlayStation game, Adolph Jr. shot his friend in the head accidentally, killing him instantly. Adolph's wife ran into the bedroom and completely lost it. Junior was arrested and is now doing hard time.

After the shooting Adolph's drinking took off, and in combination with his prescription of valium, he became a walking zombie. I told him of my situation and we made a promise to pray for each other, still do.

Sometimes life is like fighting off a Great White Shark. But ya still gotta fight!

Street Junkie

One morning in the butt-hut at the New Jersey rehab, I got there early while it was still a little dark. A new guy named Andrue, somewhere in his 30's, was rooting around in the trashcan looking for a smokable left over cigarette butt. He whipped his head around, a little embarrassed.

I didn't mean to startle him. He didn't see me and didn't know I was watching him. I gave him a Black & Mild cigar, and by the look on his face, when he lit up you'd have thought it was worth a million bucks. He smiled like a crescent moon. No teeth.

He was a junkie and you could tell he was feeling (and looking) real bad and scared too. The only clothes he had were the ones he had on, and they were filthy. So I gave him a couple of shirts. His sister had kicked him out four days ago, and he'd been on the streets until someone from family services brought him here last night. He was from the area and he had been in rehabs before, just to detox, and then he would go back out on the streets.

I told him my story about how my wife won't speak to me and how grateful I am for the chance to get sober. I was already there for six days, and was just starting to "see the light". I was still petrified, however, about the nightmare of losing the love of my life.

Andrue said, "Man, I thought I was hurtin'." He had lost his girlfriend to an overdose, but said he didn't really love her, anyway. I almost puked. Heartless fucker!

I found out later that he walked off and hitched a ride back to his sister's house. He snuck into her garage and hung himself from a doorknob with monofilament fishing line. They found him when his nephew tried to get into the garage, but Andrue's body had pinned the door shut. By the time they forced the door open, Andrue's head was only held onto his body by his spinal cord. The line had cut all the way through his neck.

Really freaked the kid out. You get numb to hearing shit like that in rehab early on.

Really hard sometimes.

An Appetite For Death

When Deveaux showed up at rehab she was a total fuckin' mess. Just out of detox from somewhere out near Chicago. She had been living on the streets for a while.

After a few days of hangin' out alone, chain smoking Marlboro Lights and staring off into the sky, she finally opened up a little bit one day at the tables. Seems she was a crackhead with a weakness for opiates too. Like most of us she liked her booze, also.

She said her detox was horrible physically. It was also real hard on her emotionally because she couldn't stop the self-loathing, hating herself for losing her two children, who were now legally with her in-laws.

Her husband had OD'd on heroin 9 months earlier. Deveaux had no world left. No hope. You could see it in her eyes and hear it in her voice. Back in Chicago, she was accidently found by paramedics (a miracle) who were there on a on a different call to the same crack house. As they were walking through the house, they saw blood flowing out from under a door. They looked inside and there was Deveaux sitting on the floor, her back to the wall, unconscious.

Both of her ankles were bleeding from her slicing them all the way around with the rusty razor blade still in her limp hand. The guy they had come for originally was already deader than hell. A bullet in the head will usually do that. They took Deveaux to the hospital.

When she regained consciousness she was overcome with sadness because she was still alive. She became deeply depressed, and kept asking the nurses to "please, please, please let me die." Oh yeah, she had tried to kill herself twice before by slitting her wrists, and fucked that up both times. That's why she tried the blade on her ankles this time.

I didn't get to know her all that well, but when I left rehab she was still pretty bad. Personally, I don't think she'll make it.

Then again, I've learned to believe in miracles!

An Eye For A Nose

I met Mark at an AA meeting in South Florida after I was out of rehab and in a halfway house. We were about the same age. He seemed like a nice enough guy, and he was wearing a wedding ring. Like me.

We started bullshitting in the parking lot while the rest of the guys were busy trying to hit on chicks. Come to find out he was from Wisconsin and took rehab instead of jail for breaking his wife's nose and collarbone during an alcohol and cocaine induced fight. Just one of his many episodes that had gotten a lot more frequent during the last 2 years with Mark.

Progression, a worsening of frequency and severity, is a very common occurrence among alcoholics and addicts who do not or will not seek help.

I asked him what the eye patch he was wearing was all about. He said his teenage stepdaughter stabbed him in the eye with a salad fork during the fight he was having that night with his wife in the kitchen. She had already called 911, and a few minutes later Mark was in the back of an ambulance. And later, in front of a judge.

He blames his obsession to get fucked up all the time on a broken family with a stepdad who was physically and emotionally abusive to his mother and him. Mark wants his life, and his wife back. He's now in the right place, a terrific rehab with great therapists and counselors and techs.

Time will tell. You just never know.

His goals are a lot like mine. We clicked.

9 Lives

Anthony tried to take himself out by slashing his neck, looking for the jugular, but missed. Thirty three stitches there and 21 more on the inside and outside of his left wrist. He was high on crystal meth and heroin pushed through his body with red blood mixed with eighty proof Hennessy Whiskey.

He had tried real hard to straighten his life out, but couldn't do it, so he finally said fuck it and decided that dying was the only sure way to escape the hell of addiction and getting high against his own fuckin' will.

Two years before that day when he cut his neck and wrist, Anthony laid his left leg across the railroad tracks and waited for the train that runs through his little Indiana town every other night. His leg was severed just below the knee and he was hoping he'd bleed to death, but his screams that came about 20 seconds later, when the pain kicked in, could be heard a block away. He couldn't suppress them.

Two guys heard him and jumped in their pick-up truck and hauled ass down to where Anthony was bellowing like a coyote caught in a bear trap. They put him in the bed of their truck and Anthony was almost floating in his own blood by the time they got him to the hospital.

Emergency surgery saved him "for some reason" as Anthony likes to put it. His neck and wrist have ugly scars and he was still getting used to his fake leg when I first met him.

I said, "Hey bro" and lit him a cigarette. He looked at me, took a moment to smile and said, "Thanks dude." His eyes were still puffy from his last run with booze and dope, and it looked like he'd been crying a little.

This fuckin' disease has really beat him up. He still wants to get high, but he knows the next run will surely kill him and for now, he wants to live again. Good therapists and the 12 steps of AA and NA can do that for him.

But addiction is strong and cunning.

We put out our cigarettes and went into the big room for the morning big-group therapy session.

Anthony's life is another awesome calamity of the cold world of addiction, but his miracle is happening. He's in a great rehab with a tender, loving therapist with great expertise. I hope and pray Anthony comes out the other side.

Accidents Happen

I walked out and down to the picnic tables for coffee and smokes before this day in rehab would unfold in earnest. Harry, a guy with a severe limp and a nasty oxy habit, who looked something like Kirk Douglas did when he was 40 years old, bummed a Newport off of me (no more Black & Milds).

I'd never really talked to Harry before and he hadn't told his story to the group, so I knew very little about him. Harry brought out his lighter and lit his cigarette and mine. Rocky the squirrel came over and Harry said it reminded him of home. Me too.

Anyway, Harry asked me what my deal was. I told him. Everybody I've ever met in the 2 rehabs I've been in seems to have an incredible story, with peaks and valleys to the extreme.

Then, Harry told me that the oxys had almost killed him and had left him broke and without his locksmith business. Seems Harry was also an alcoholic (a jello-shot or a double-shot is but a KILL shot for an alcoholic) along with the oxys.

Four years ago Harry fell off of his horse, broke his femur and injured his hip. Two years after that, he was run over by a car. The two guys in the car, stopped, got out and proceeded to throw Harry in the trunk. They dumped his body on the side of a back road near Atlantic City, NJ, where an elderly woman ironically with the same last name as Harry's, spotted him and called 911. They never caught the guys.

Anyway, Harry was great the last time I spoke with him. He's really into the program and I'm pretty sure he's gonna make it and stay clean.

He had a great therapist. An earth Angel.

Fuckin Weird

Mac is a cool little Italian guy that I met in the south Jersey rehab and we wound up together again in at the same south Florida rehab about two weeks apart. I was there first. Knowing how he looked in Jersey and now seeing him here, I could tell he was doing much better.

It's not easy recovering from twenty plus years of hard alcohol addiction, as well as coke and meth. Along with the fact that he was still facing another operation to "fix" his scalp, my buddy Mac was doin' pretty damn good.

Not long before showing up in rehab, Mac and some of his buddies in Staten Island, NY, were so strung out after several days of tweaking (meth, speeding) and drinking, they got into a bizarre fight using bic lighters as little swords and knives. They fought among themselves and Mac says, "we were so tweaked out, it all seemed proper, like it was meant to be or something.

Fuckin' weird, huh Nel?" Well, nothing's weird to me anymore.

Anyway, after a couple of the guys and girls noticed that Mac was unconscious, they decided to set his hair on fire. After the flame and melting skin got out of control, one of the girls got scared and wrapped Mac's head in a leather jacket and put the fire out. Some of his hair will never grow back and some of the scarring will remain, but hey, could've been worse.

Just saw Mac a few days ago. He was on his way to chair an NA meeting in Boca Rotan. He is doing fabulous.

He got lucky, and so did I. Great rehabs and therapists. And a forgiving God!

THE TWO MICE

Two mice fell into a bucket of cream.

One mouse gave up and quickly drowned.

The second mouse struggled so hard that he churned the cream into butter and crawled out.

I am that mouse.

"Feeling better. Three months clean and sober."
Miami, FL – 2009

PART III:
IN THEIR OWN WORDS

"THE DARKER THE NIGHT, THE BRIGHTER THE DAY"

Paul (South Dakota)

I found out about alcohol by taking sips from my mom and dad's beer at backyard parties when I was about 10 years old. That's when I knew how much I liked the feeling of beer. When they had friends over to play cards, my twin sister and I would sneak bottles of beer from the cooler they used to keep the beer and soda cold.

By the time I was 12, I was sneaking beer, wine, or whiskey any time I could. Even then I already knew that I liked getting drunk more than the other kids, including my sister. It was a private little thing I did and I could even act straight around people and they couldn't tell I was buzzed.

By the time I was 17, I felt like a pro because I knew an older guy who would buy me beer if I showed him naked pictures of my sister. I had a lot of them because she said she felt like a model when I took naked pictures of her.

I had my first accident in my dad's truck and the cops couldn't even tell that I was drunk. I told them I had to swerve so I wouldn't hit a deer. It will be 15 years next month that I drove my Ford Bronco into the Skittle River that runs just outside of our town, and my three best friends drowned. But I got out.

For the past 15 years all I have been doing is drinking and taking depression medicine, but nothing can stop the nightmares about the accident, and the guilt and shame that is always with me. This is the 3rd rehab I've been in to try and quit getting high and drunk.

I will be 33 years old on the anniversary of the accident, but I feel like I'm at least 100.

My liver is almost gone and I am very close to having wet brain (whatever that is), so if I don't get better this time, fuck it.

I should have died with my guy's that night anyway. Help!

This is the best rehab yet. My therapist is so kind, and he understands me. He's had many problems too in his life. Now I know that I was not ready when I was in the other rehabs. I am starting to think that Jesus really loves me and forgives me, and I want to stay sober for him and my therapist, and for me. My mom and sister too. And also for my dad up in heaven.

I miss my dog, but my mom says he is waiting for me.

My friend Ruthie helped me write this.

The darker the night, the brighter the day, she says. Hope Ruthie is right.

Marguarite (Mexico)

Hello. My name is Marguarite, I am 37 years old. I have been drinking every day for the last 21 years. My step-father, Enrico, got me drunk the night of my sweet sixteen birthday party, and then raped me while my mom was at work, and after my girlfriends went home.

He said he would kill my dog, Shampoo, and then tell my mom that I climbed into bed with him and starting kissing him if I ever told anybody. I let him screw me for the next 12 years, but I always got drunk first, and he got me vodka and mixed it with orange juice, and I'd pretend that I was dreaming while he was doing it to me.

I finally told my brother, Ricky, who lived with my real dad, and he told my real dad about Enrico. My dad came over and got into a fight with Enrico, and Enrico said that it was my idea, and that I had told him that I loved him. I started screaming and my dad shot Enrico in the stomach with his pistol.

Ricky called 911 and my dad drove away and all I could do was keep on screaming. Ricky was going crazy.

Then the ambulance came and they took Enrico to the hospital. He got better, and when he came home he never raped my again.

My dad got arrested at my mom-mom's house in New York and he is still in prison for a few more years.

I kept drinking until my mom had a surprise intervention for me last year. I said OK and went to rehab. I have not had a drink now for 13 months and I feel so much better that I never want to go back to vodka again.

My therapist in rehab saved my life and I still talk to her on the phone at least 3 times a week. I have a partner now, she is my soul mate, I think. She was my sponsor in AA and we fell in love and I got a job at the Ritz Carlton as a waitress, and I really love it there.

I am so happy now that I thank God every morning and every night for my sobriety, and my new life. I visit my dad once a month and I haven't seen Enrico for over a year. I call my mom once in a while.

I think she knew all along about Enrico. I hated her, now I've forgiven her because that is a part of the AA way of life.

Jasper (Louisiana)

I was born, and grew up in a small town about 30 miles north of New Orleans. My mom's aunt, my great aunt, was killed because she was in the wrong place at the wrong time at a convenience store that was being robbed.

I had a pretty normal childhood, but I never felt like I fit in, even with my family.

We were an athletic family, and I was pretty good at baseball, basketball and football. But I never really liked sports as much as reading and drawing pictures. I even had a couple of my pencil sketches displayed in a glass case at my high school. One was of my mom and dad kissing (before they got divorced), and the other one was of my horse, Dandy.

Dandy was definitely my best friend. He's getting old now, so instead of riding him, I walk him out through the meadow and down to the creek.

My last year of high school, the year my folks got divorced, my friends Zeke and Rebel turned me on to crystal meth, out in the woods in Rebel's jeep. They said it was the same kind of meth that Adolph Hitler and his generals used during WWII. Good shit!

We snorted 2 lines each off of Rebel's dashboard, and from that moment on for the next 2 ½ years, I lived on cigarettes, beer, and crystal meth. At first, it was like my dream come true, the greatest feeling in the world, and it made me feel comfortable with people and inspired me to draw and paint more.

I lost 48 pounds, my teeth started to rot, and I had a meth induced heart attack when I was 21. I detoxed while I was in the hospital.

A pastor, also a heart patient, introduced me to Jesus Christ. He talked me into checking into a rehab in South Florida. I signed up for the Christian track. My primary therapist was named Marlene. She was a former addict herself.

My story is not very exciting, but I can tell you that Marlene, the big book, the 12 steps, and God saved me from certain death. I am very grateful.

A miracle.

I hope somebody reading this will reach out for help just like I did.

There will be somebody there like Marlene. She is not the only caring therapist out there. So, please don't be afraid to save your life and your soul by reaching out for help.

Lynette (Connecticut)

My ugly story of alcohol and drug abuse began on a Saturday
morning when my mom shot my dad to death after taking a
beating from him the night before. On almost every Friday night
my dad would come home after drinking and partying and beat the
hell out of my mom.

Mom had had her nose broken twice, broken ribs, broken fingers
and some of her hair pulled out on many occasions. My dad would
always yell at her and tell her she was fat, ugly and dumb.

My sister and I had talked about killing him, almost like it was a
fantasy that could never come true but was fun talking about. But
on this one Saturday morning my mom shot him 4 times in the
chest when he was passed out on the couch.

My sister and I were at cheerleading practice out on the big field at
the high school. My Nana on my mom's side came to practice
early and picked us up. My sister and I knew right away that
something must have happened. Nana had a bottle of brandy and
some of her nerve pills for us. We didn't know why she came to
get us but we both had a feeling that my dad had killed my mom.
What a relief it was to find out it was the other way around. Hip-
Hip Hurray !

Nana drove us to the county hospital where there was a
policeman standing outside my mom's door. The doctor told us
that she had been in shock and he had given her something to
sleep. I remember feeling light and high from the brandy and pills

Nana gave me. From that day on I was definitely addicted to that feeling.

So I chased that euphoric feeling for the next 21 years. But no matter how much I drank or what kind of dope I did, seldom could I find that feeling again. I was miserable and sick, both mentally and physically. I would not even eat for fear it would screw up whatever buzz I had going. All I did was drink, do drugs and smoke Kool cigarettes.

Cutting to the chase, my sister and her husband talked me into going into a rehab facility where my detox was horrible, pure hell for a few days. That was over 2 years ago and I am so grateful that I can never possibly thank my sister and brother-in-law enough!

There are still some things I can't remember, but my therapist told me not to worry about that.

I still smoke my Kools and have switched to coffee instead of booze. In the last 2 years I've put on 35 pounds and my sister says I'm still a little too thin. Maybe that's because she's a little heavier than me. We joke about that a lot.

I'm happier now than I've ever been in my entire life. I want to say thank you to my sister, my brother-in-law and my new family in AA and NA.

Keep comin' back. It works if you work it, so work it, you're worth it.

Sean (Kentucky)

The first memory I have is of being held under the kitchen faucet by my grand-pop because I was holding my breath and turning blue. I can still feel and see the water, so cold, drenching my little face. My second memory is of waking up in the hospital at the age of 5 having vodka and orange juice pumped out of my stomach. The lights were so bright and I tried to scream but the tube was just being pulled out.

My grand-mom and grand-pop were there. They were so afraid of losing me because it would have been their fault, plus they had already lost their daughter, who was my mom, along with my dad to a car accident right after I was born. They were both drunk and my dad hit a tree.' Grand-mom and grand-pop always said that my dad was swerving to miss a dog.

My grand-mom and grand-pop were both alcoholics. My grand-pop drank beer and my grand-mom drank screwdrivers. That's what I drank when I was 5 and in the hospital. By the time I was 14 I was drinking beer every day with my grand-pop. I was also running the household and helping myself to grandma's valium and grandpa's painkillers and Librium.

They were both completely helpless when they came up with the bright idea to fake a car accident and then scam the insurance company. It didn't work and my grand-pop got a DUI and was ordered by the judge to spend 28 days in a rehab facility which was only about 5 or 10 miles from our house.

While he was in there he had a couple of seizures and then a stroke. He never came out of it and died in the hospital a few days later. Grandma ended up in a nursing home where she was heavily sedated 24-7. I wound up with the house, which was paid off.

I worked a few days a week as a house painter, the guy I worked for was a hard-core alcoholic like me. I made just enough money to pay taxes on the house and buy booze, which at this time consisted of cheap beer and vodka, straight from the bottle. Once I found out that the pain I was having in my abdomen was caused by the beginning of cirrhosis of my liver I quit drinking and my doctor helped me get into rehab after I detoxed for 10 days in the hospital.

Only by the grace of God did I take my 90 days at rehab seriously and developed a great relationship with the counselors and my primary therapist. Even though I really wanted and needed to quit drinking, I'm certain that I couldn't have done it alone.

As of now, I still go to AA meetings and will for the rest of my life. I have been chairing the local Wednesday night meetings for almost 5 years. The "Wednesday nighters" are like family to me and I love them all dearly.

I thank my higher power every morning and night for my miracle of sobriety.

Kelly (Washington State)

I was born in Seattle, Washington in 1984. I had a good childhood and neither one of my parents were drug addicts, but my dad drank a lot and this used to cause arguments between my mom and dad. They always made up though and I'm sure that they love each other very much. I have two older brothers who were both very good at sports and were also good students in school, unlike me.

I hated school. I never liked sports either. But I love animals and have wanted to be a veterinarian for as far back as I can remember. To be honest, I never felt like I fit in with my family, so I kind of flew under the radar and kept to myself, mostly in my room with my cat, Rachael.

My best friend Toni hated her parents and practically lived at my house. She cried all the time, mostly because her mom, who was thin and pretty made fun of her because she was overweight and really not that pretty. Too me she was, though. Toni is a beautiful person.

Toni and I would sit up in my room with my window open and smoke pot and talk about everything and listen to music. We started drinking Sambuca and I really, really liked the way it made me feel, especially in combination with smoking pot. Toni liked it too, but not as much as I did. It got to the point where I never wanted to leave my room. I was drinking and smoking pot all the time.

I would get stoned when I woke up and keep smoking all day and then start on my Sambuca. My brother Nick would get us the Sambuca and Toni would give him a hand job every once in a while for getting it for us. I thought it was disgusting, but I really counted on my Sambuca and sometimes white wine. My mom took me to the doctors because she thought I was depressed and the doctor prescribed Zoloft and later on switched me to Xanax and Cymbalta.

Well, between the pot, the booze and the Xanax, I was pretty much in my own little heaven. And became even more of a recluse. I started smoking cigarettes and told my mom that they helped me overcome my depression and also made me calmer on the inside. Toni was even fed up with me at his point and she quit coming over. So I isolated in my room for at least 3 years.

Anytime my mom, dad or even my brother Nick who was still living at home, said anything negative about my behavior, I would cry and say that I felt like killing myself, so they would back off and leave me alone. When Nick moved out and moved into an apartment with Toni, I would have the house to myself on most week days and that's when I would venture out of my room and walk around the house carrying Rachael and go from window to window looking outside for God knows what or who. I was so strung out that I didn't even go to my grandmother's viewing or funeral when she died and I loved her sooooo much, too!

The day of her funeral I drank so much that I was drunk by noon and took about a half a bottle of Xanax. I just wanted to sleep and forget about everything. I was so ashamed of myself that I didn't care if I lived or died. When my parents got home from the funeral, they found me unconscious in my room. The door was open, good thing, because if it was closed they never would have seen me.

I woke up in the hospital and I felt so sick, it was horrible. I went into a seizure two times and almost died both times. After 10 days in the hospital I flew directly to a rehab facility in California. I never even got to go home and see Rachael.

Well, for the first time in about 5 years I was facing life on life's terms. Hard, hard, hard. But it got better. My therapist is the miracle worker that gave me my life back. I was learning how to laugh and feel emotions for the first time in ages.

When my 60 days at rehab were over, I didn't want to leave. So, I went to a half-way house for girls only, and now I am the on-site house manager. I have my own little apartment there and they even let me have Rachael with me after I pleaded with them and convinced them that having Rachael there would help in my recovery. And it did really help a lot and everybody loved Rachael.

When my year is up here, I'm going to go to school in Washington state and study to become a veterinarian. Life is good again. I really can't thank my parents and my therapists enough for giving my life back to me. I also thank God every morning and every night for working this miracle into my life.

Rehab gave me a second chance at life, and I love it! But I'll always have to watch it, because this disease is sneaky and vicious.

Terrance (Illinois)

I don't remember my first drink, but I remember the first time I got drunk. Not real drunk but tipsy enough to get hooked on the feeling of alcohol. Rodney, Steve, Kenny and me drove to an away high school football game and it was real cold with the wind blowing in from Lake Michigan. We were in Rodney's black 4 door Chevy Impala.

We were all 17 except for Rodney, he was about 18 or 19 and looked really old for his age so he was able to buy beer in a couple of bars in our town so we all chipped in and got a quart of beer each and a 6 pack of beer in bottles. Everything was in bottles back then. Not like today. We all had a beer by the time we got to the game except for Rodney. We watched about 2 plays of the football game and then went back to the car to drink beer, get warm and listen to the radio.

We were all starting to feel pretty good from the beer when Steve (who I was sitting next to) rolled down the back window and held up his fingers in a peace sign and said "peace brother" and a guy with black leather gloves on punched him in the mouth and knocked one of his top front teeth out. I spit a mouthful of beer out and started laughing and I can still see Steve holding his mouth with one hand and reaching up front with the other hand for Rodney to give him a napkin for the blood and his tooth.

Well anyway that was the beginning of my love and hate affair with alcohol. Especially beer but I would drink anything. It didn't take long before I was smoking weed and hash, and snorting coke whenever some came along. But I never bought any coke.

After about 15 years of drinking almost every day, I got so sick of it I started going to Alcoholics Anonymous meetings in the next town over. I thought I had it beat after about 6 months and quit my meetings, which in reality I enjoyed and missed. A couple months later I went down to my local bar for one mug of beer and that turned into another 6 years of drinking, this time only worse than before.

I switched over from Budweiser to vodka and got to the point where I was drinking every day and night, sometimes even a swig or two in the morning before work to get feeling right. Normal I guess.

My wife and mom, who lived with us, were pretty understanding until I started losing my temper when they said anything about the vodka. That's when they talked me into going into rehab. I wanted to quit and I knew I could not go on that way forever. So they took me over to a small rehab center up north and I detoxed there for 8 days.

The first 5 days were the worst days of my life. And then I went by plane to another rehab, a lot bigger and stayed for 45 days. It was the best and smartest thing I ever did in my life. My therapists and the friends I made there gave me my life back.

Even though I wanted to get sober, I never really thought it would happen for me. At first I really went for my wife and mom, and then I found out that I had to focus on myself before I could do anything for them. So I did what they told me at rehab and they were right. I wish I could say their names here!

I still go to meetings and call or see my sponsor once a week, mostly on Saturdays. If it wasn't for rehab I would either be crazy or dead. My liver was going bad but it's ok now, my wife is happy and proud and when my mom died I was sober so she was happy and proud of me, too. I hope you can't see these tears, but I started drinking again about 4 months ago. My wife wants me to go back to rehab. I don't know. Damn it to hell!

Richard (Kansas)

Hello, my name is Richard and I was born on March 14th, 1971 in Wichita Kansas. My story of addiction didn't start because of my parents or heredity or nothing like that. My parents didn't do anything except smoke cigarettes and serve wine on Christmas when my aunt and uncle came over. My grandmother was there too until she died, she would usually drink a few glasses of wine, too.

I would go around and take sips out of everybody's wine for as far back as I can remember. And all year long I would think about how good the wine made me feel at Christmas. So, when I was about 14, my best friend, Tim and I stole the Christmas wine from my parents and went out behind the middle school bleachers and drank a quart bottle of the stuff and I felt great for a while and then Tim got sick and threw up and that made me throw up. I remember my throat hurt for a while after that.

Tim got some pot when we were about 16 just about to turn 17 and we smoked a joint out behind the bleachers. We got really high and went back to his house and stole a small bottle of vodka from his dad's workshop. That was an awesome day, the day I should have realized that I had an addictive personality because right then and there I knew I had to feel that way every day or I would get agitated and do anything to get any kind of a buzz. I even drank chloraseptic sore throat medicine one time that I got from the bathroom medicine cabinet at Tim's house because it had some alcohol in it. Talk about fuckin' sick. I thought I was gonna die.

As soon as I got my driver's license it was all over, I had a car that my uncle sold to me for 200 bucks. So I got this guy, who was 22, to buy me beer and I always gave him one out of the pack. I got pot too, that was easy, and I started smoking cigarettes to cover up the pot smell from my parents, especially my mom.

I got a DUI coming back from partying in the woods with a bunch of guys and girls, I had pot on me but the cops never found it. They called my dad and he was really mad. Scary mad. And when I got home my mom was crying and that really made me sad.

When I was about 22 or 23 Tim and a guy he met in college turned me on to crystal meth and gave me 2 valium to take when I wanted to come down or we ran out of crystal. Man I thought I had died and went straight to heaven. I had found the love of my life. I started doing crystal every day, it was cheap and easy to get. I also had the valium thing down.

I still smoked pot and drank but crystal and valium were my babies. When my teeth started rotting out, instead of quitting crystal, I had all my teeth pulled out and got false ones, top and bottom. I had a decent job by then but they started random drug testing and I failed the first one I had and I could have gone to treatment for 28 days and kept my job, but I said to myself, why should I, I have no intention of quitting crystal for these cocksuckers.

So I finally got unemployment and spent every nickel on drugs. I was still at my parent's house and I thought they had basically given up on talking to me about my habits anymore and I liked that. I had an outside door that led straight to my bedroom which was in the basement and I never really had to see my mom and dad.

Then one day when I got out of bed at about noon or 1 o'clock. My dad came down and said he wanted me to come upstairs for a minute. I felt like shit and I needed a couple lines and a couple of beers, so after that, I went upstairs and there was my mom, my aunt and uncle, my 2 cousins and this lady and man who said they wanted to help me and asked me to go to treatment to try and quit my booze and drugs. I was totally stunned and I said, "Hell no and fuck you," and practically ran out to my car, but my dad had parked behind me so I couldn't get out of the driveway.

I was totally pissed and scared. Scared because there was no way I could live without crystal. No way. I called Tim and that traitor told me he knew about the intervention and agreed with my parents that I needed help or I was gonna die.

When I started crystal I weighed 192 lbs. By now I weighed about 150 and I thought I looked great, especially with my new teeth...so I took my bike and rode to my dealers house and then, behind the bleachers. I was sitting there on the ground high as hell when Tim drove back there and started telling me that I was gonna die probably within a year if I didn't get to treatment and quit the drugs, especially crystal.

But when he told me that this had been killing my mother for a long time and I didn't even realize it, I did 4 lines of crystal and 1/2 pint of vodka and said let's go. So we put my bike in his trunk and went back to my house and everybody was still there and my dad was holding my mom because she was crying so hard.

I went over and kissed my mom on the cheek and promised her I would give rehab a shot...well that was 17 months ago. I spent 60 days at rehab and fell in love with being straight. I'm happy, and I'm up to 187 lbs. And I have a great new relationship with my parents.

I'm still in a half way house and I think I'm gonna stay here for another few months and then get my own place. I've had a job for 3 months at a hotel doing valet parking. I love it and I don't have to worry about piss and hair tests anymore. That in itself is worth shouting about.

Well, all I can say is, "If I can do it, anybody can," and I recommend it. You just have to hand it all over to your higher power and the people God puts in your life. Like my therapists, they are special people and they WILL help you kick this ruthless monster's ass if you let them! Thank you for letting me tell my story. Hope it helps somebody. It helped me.

Raynetta (Mississippi)

I told Mister Nelson that my story is a little sad but not too interesting, but he said he cared about me and I should tell it to make me feel better if I wanted to. I said yes sir. Mister Nelson is the only man who ever said he cared about me.

Little old Raynetta, nobody ever give two shits 'bout me. All I know is my daddy's buddy friends started giving me whisky and wine when I was about twelve years old. I got drunk and they laughed and raped me in the back barn of my horse Billy's by our stream. Raynetta hated the whiskey at first, but after a while that whisky tasted better and better to me.

They came every Friday night to get drunk and come callin' on me. I fooled them and got drunk before they even come back to that bad back barn, Billy's barn. I was taking care of my horse Billy one night when the bad nasty men came callin' on me and started laughin' and wanting me to take off my black dress. I ran to Billy and screamed and he jumped and bit my finger off. The nasty, bad men must've got scared and they ran away.

My aunt Toolie slapped me and her own eyes popped out cause I was drunk and missing a finger, so she made me drink some more whisky and poured whisky on my finger hole and tied it up with barn rags.

I ran away the next day to the city forever when my daddy took Billy out in our stream and shot him in his head, and my Billy fell down and rolled down our stream to the waterfall dam next to the city. So that is where I went to.

I got my own whisky in the city and made five dollars for suckie and ten dollars for my pussy, and a man Joey took me in. We smoked crack and Joey said it will make me feel better. All the time I loved that crack. Joey gave me whisky, cigarettes and crack and a nice bed.

I had to make one hundred dollars every day for Joey and he bought me nice dresses and shoes. One day I came back to Joey with two hundred dollars happy, but Joey was dead and even his eyes was still open. I cried and ran to the police hall and a nice woman named Nancy talked to me.

Nancy took me to a church and then to a new place where I can get better (a rehab). I cried and was sick for two weeks then Mister Nelson came from Florida to see me and tell me that I am a good person of the world. Mister Nelson gave me a bible and an AA big book but had to leave. Thank you, Mister Nelson.

I miss and love my Billy, not Joey.

Jim (Arizona)

Today I pretty much lay in bed all day. It's what I usually do these days. I think I have stepped into a bear trap that I can't get my foot out of, and I haven't hollered for help much yet. I know I probably need help to get out. I have resorted to spending almost all my earnings on this drug, I went as far as spending change for half a pill today, nothing special though.

I have abandoned myself from a ride, because I would rather spend my money on one day's worth of a high, in what time I neglect the person who would be hurt the most, the one that cares, name, understood. It hurts to the point where I would rather write this instead of it. Nuff said.

I can't believe I fell victim to the thing I hated most. It blows, but at the same time it feels soo good, I feel as though I'm on a downwards spiral, and am afraid that when I go back to work and have more money to blow, I probably will, I really Don't want to but I feel I may. This is almost all I think about... This habit, addiction, disease?

I have the meds to stop without withdrawal, but I Don't take them as prescribed I need to get help and let someone know, but in a way I'm scared to. I Don't want to tell Nicole I'm using again and I'm afraid to tell my mom because she already has stuff to worry about and I Don't want her to be on me more because she already thinks I'm always doing something bad, I Don't know, I have mixed feelings about this subject.

Jody (Pennsylvania)

Out of all of my friends, I was the last one that anybody would have expected to not be successful in life. After all, I was pretty, smart and athletic. There was nothing I couldn't do or overcome.

But I was no match for ecstasy. From the very first time I tried it I was ecstatic. Ecstatic over ecstasy. Very funny, huh? My boyfriend said I liked it too much. Ecstasy made me feel totally free for the first time in my life. No inhibitions, no worries about college or what my parents expected out of me.

Ecstasy had gone from a weekend party drug to an everyday thing. I never drank unless I was doing ecstasy. I didn't think I could even talk to people without the help of ecstasy.

I was smart enough to know that I was in trouble. I couldn't live without ecstasy and I couldn't live with it. I decided one day after running out for a few days and not being able to find some, that the best way to end this whole major problem was to kill myself.

So I filled the bath tub, got in and tried to slice my wrists. After the first one and all the blood, I freaked out and called my boy friend and he came over and took me to the hospital. By the time the doctors got done with me, my boy friend had told my parents and the doctors everything.

My mom and dad had read about every damn drug in the book except ecstasy. They were really scared and I felt so pitiful about putting them through all of this. I didn't like what I saw in my dad's eyes. He was heartbroken.

The doctor had explained to them that ecstasy was not a physically addictive drug like heroin, pain killers or benzos. More of a compulsion and psychologically addiction. Something like pot is to some people. Whatever it is, ecstasy, especially when it came to music, dancing, sex, conversation and even wine...it had me. Mind, body and soul.

When I left the hospital instead of going home, my parents drove me across to a facility where I spent 3 days talking to counselors and a psychiatrist. After that I was driven to the airport in a van and flown to a rehab in Florida. That changed my life.

I got to know some of the most wonderful people there that I had ever met in my life. Not only were the therapists and techs awesome, but the clients (patients) themselves.

To this day, 3 years after we met there, Nancy and I are best friends. She is married and I am engaged to my soul-mate who I met in rehab. I am a new person. A much better person because of rehab, especially my primary therapist, Wanda. Ecstasy is a thing of the past for me. Now I'm ecstatic about life!

I had fun writing this. Thank you. Pray for me and I'll Pray for you. Deal?

Edward (Georgia)

I was born on July 30, 1976 in Augusta, Georgia. My parents were married and were 28 years old. My father is a pecan farmer. I have one older sister by 2 years. My early to middle childhood was burdensome. I could never seem to please my father. He spanked me a lot with a leather belt, and my mother would often be dragged between my father and me in our conflict.

I remember taking a drink of coca-cola in a steak restaurant for the first time when I was 2 years old, and feeling a caffeine rush which I liked. When I was in 10th grade, I transferred to a prep school and worked very hard academically for the next 3 years. When I was 17 I went to Harvard summer school and had a great time hanging out in our apartment style dorm with the other guys and girls until the wee hours of the morning.

That was the first time I encountered crystal meth. I wondered how they stayed up all night playing cards when I went to bed at 2am, and finally they let me in on their secret and offered me a half a gram, but I refused because I knew I would probably want more afterward. Two years later at UVA I gave in to temptation.

When I graduated from high school I had a full scholarship to Tulane in New Orleans, but my father pressured me into attending the University of Virginia instead. I tried to please him by attending UVA, but I was miserable there.

I started taking Prozac at UVA in 1994 and spent my nights in the 24 hour dormitory computer lab with the new world wide web. I didn't rush a fraternity because I wasn't confident enough, but I constantly craved alcohol so much that I had a hard time abstaining.

I went to UVA for a year and had a 3.7 GPA, but then the next summer I took 4 hits of LSD with my cousin in Athens, GA. It was some of the strongest acid I have ever taken. After the trip, I lay in bed for 6 months in a depressive state at home, and I dropped out of college.

I transferred to UGA the next winter and dove into the drug scene. I was so happy to be home again, but I was really manic. I smoked marijuana, took ecstasy, and snorted cocaine for the first time. Then my parents had me hospitalized and I was furious. I went to UGA on and off from 1995 to 2001, when I finally graduated with a BS in chemistry.

During this time I did huge amounts of expensive drugs such as MDMA, LSD, cocaine, marijuana, and crystal meth. I had one more nervous breakdown from crystal meth while working as a patient transporter at a local hospital.

During this time I drove from Athens to Atlanta to party at nightclubs and raves in Atlanta. I danced a lot and learned to love techno dance music. I had some unbelievably ecstatic transcendental moments there and even saw Madonna one night at a club.

When I finally graduated from UGA in December, 2001, I got a job as a quality control coordinator at a local pharmaceutical plant in

Gainesville. I rented a old big house in Athens and had a steady girlfriend, plus a best friend/drug buddy as well.

All of that fell apart when I was fired from my job after acting crazy at work after a Ketamine binge. I moved back home to the farm in 2003 and took Zyprexa, which knocked me out, for a few years while working on the farm for my dad. I still drove to Atlanta on the weekends and used crystal meth there, too.

In 2006, I became paranoid, packed up all my stuff into my RAV4 and drove cross country and back. My father started constantly having me committed into GA Regional for 10 days, a public mental institution, over and over during these years, but the hospital always let me out after a week or so because they said I was "highly functional."

I never got rehired after my 2006 trip, and then I lived off of my credit cards in our extra farmhouse, with my new roommate Jason, whom I had met recently in GA Regional, and was from Macon. Jason and I started doing a lot of crystal meth and later IV cocaine until I went to jail and he went to rehab.

After that he moved to Maine to live with a girl whom he met on the internet. I was very lonely last year in my farmhouse without Jason and I started smoking crack cocaine to cope with my life. My father caught on and started clamping down seriously on me. I didn't have a job and neither of my parents wanted me staying with them in their home.

Last month I confronted my father. He had me sent to jail and that's how I wound up with you here today in rehab.

Kerry (New York)

I have been contemplating my psyche for the last few days.

My drunkenness usually precludes me from such melancholy thought or invention. In my mind I am buried six feet underground.

Encased in a six foot by three foot box. It is not dark because there is a light and surprisingly oxygen is being supplied but I AM trapped.

I cannot move.

Even though there is light I cannot see myself due to the tight confinement of the box. I can wiggle but there is NO escape!

Soon death will come, my body needs to be delivered from this pit but my mind and spirit are also captured and tormented by do's and don'ts, haves and have not's, questions, answers, mistakes, gains and losses.

I am weary now and ready to sleep, but I know that sleep will come at a cost.

Sorrow and pain to some, a passing NOD of ambivalence to others........Nonetheless, let it come!

Amy (Ohio)

"How did she get out of there?" exclaimed the inattentive hospital staff. I was close to the hospital emergency exit door, ready to run, somewhere. I was told I had a sly smirk and a look of accomplishment, for I had managed to somehow wiggle my wrists out of the restraints. That was the second time in a matter of a few minutes that I had nearly escaped whatever treatment I was about endure. They called me Houdini.

I had taken what was left of my Prozac and alprazolam and probably about five shots of rum. I just wanted the pain to go away. I didn't really want to die; I just could not handle the depth of depression one more minute.

This was not my first attempt. Last time I had my stomach pumped and I had tubes shoved down my throat. People who try to commit suicide are those who do are not capable of thinking past the pain in most instances. I didn't think about my husband, my children, and grandchildren. I just wanted the freaking pain to leave me the hell alone. I was 50 years old.

I was having a very rough time dealing with the fact that my X, so-called husband of 20 years had been arrested for being a pedophile. We had been divorced a few years and he had remarried. His step-daughter told on him. What an extremely brave little ten year old girl. In his confession, he admitted to having molested children in several states. There were about 30 or more children, including my six children, but because it had happened so many years ago and because so many of the victims didn't want to talk about it, he was only charged on the crimes against one precious little girl.

How could I not have known? I hated myself with a deep hatred that is very hard to describe. I loathed myself.

What made it so horrific was the fact that this imbecile, this bastard, had tricked me for many years. He was a con-artist and liar among many other horrible things.

At a very young age, a gullible teenager (me) believed a "prophet" that I was to marry this man and that we were to sing together in the 'ministry.' I always had a heart to sing. I have been singing in public since I was about five years old. I Don't feel normal if I am not singing.

Come to find out, many years later, I was told that a family friend of mine heard this woman 'prophet' tell the story of how this man paid her to give that 'prophesy' to me. This person, I cannot call him a man, I call him dirty boy, had developed and carried out an elaborate plan.

We ended up having a "children's ministry." He built a fabulous stage, I painted the scenery, I learned to use puppets, wrote skits, and put on quite a production. We even sang together.

I put my whole heart and soul into it. The very children that I was trying to lead to God, he was trying to find a way to get an opportunity to molest. We taught children's church in a few different churches. The enormity of the travesty unfolded in my mind like unending fireworks.

There were always children around our house. My six children had lots of friends, but one by one, they seemed to not want to come over anymore. I was puzzled. He always said that our children's friends should stay over at our house because "you don't know what the other children's parents are like." One night I heard a commotion, I found him in Diana's room leaning over her. He said that someone had a nightmare and I went back to sleep.

The marriage was filled with neglect, verbal abuse and later on physical abuse by this person. I was told I was stupid and that no man would ever want me. I cried inside night after night wondering what it was about me that made him not want to have sex with me. I would go on crazy diets, I tried fixing my makeup differently, and I tried to allure him. Instead, he would sit in his rocking chair in the living room reading a book and many times staring out into space.

I didn't realize he was fucking the children. Now I know and understand that it had nothing to do with some unknown flaw that I possessed but rather it was because I didn't fit his perverted sexual criteria. I wasn't young enough and I didn't look like a child anymore. I was a woman.

One day when Diana was being a bit obstinate, he screamed at me over and over to get a belt and whip my 11 year old Diana, and I refused. He punched me and I went flying backwards across the hallway. The shame was more painful than the bruises. He also kept us in poverty. I couldn't work for many years because I couldn't afford a babysitter. He was in construction, but he would disappear for blocks of time that were unaccounted for. Why didn't I put the pieces together?

None of it made sense to me. I thought we were a Christian family. I thought we were supposed to be spreading God's love.

So, he was arrested and he was sentenced to 15 years in jail in South Carolina. I was relieved to know that he couldn't hurt anybody anymore, at least for a while. Some of my adult children still believed in him and 'forgave' him as he preached to them that they should do so. I knew he was pure evil and I knew that if he got out again that he would only search for his next victim. My youngest son was still living with him when he got arrested. Mark will not discuss what transpired while he was there.

My brain could not fathom how any of my children could still be on a speaking basis with him. This bothered me to the point of drinking. I was livid and angry towards God. How could he have allowed this to happen? I trusted Him. I believed that if I served Him that he would watch over us. Not wanting to hate God anymore, I turned the hatred deeply inward. The day I found out that he was released from prison only after two years, I immediately passed out. Then I became almost catatonic. I couldn't speak, I couldn't move. I felt my whole being, my soul, my essence being swiftly sucked down into a black hole. I was disappearing and I didn't know where I was going. All I could do was writing. My husband, Robert, kept saying, "Amy, Amy, Amy,

Don't leave me, I love you, come back, please come back." When I came to, I was just repeatedly saying, "He is an evil, evil man."

Struggling, dealing with this knowledge and attempting to still hold a job, I turned to alcohol to soothe the misery. Then one Christmas, a couple years later, my oldest daughter, Gina, gave me a present. After I opened it up, I saw that it was a Recovery Bible. I thought that was nice until she said," You know that is from dad, right?" I snapped inside. How could this 'dirty boy' have the audacity to send me a Bible?

How could he send it through my Gina? How could Gina not realize that this would upset me? Again, I went into a tail spin. This time, I asked my husband, Robert, to take me to the doctor for some help. She firmly suggested that I go to the mental ward in Franklin.

As soon as they put me in the little room all by myself, I literally went crazy. I tried breaking anything I could find. I wanted to die.

While in this facility, I met an art therapist. Using my art ability enabled me to express myself in ways I never could before. The psychiatrist wasn't too terrific. He put me on a litany of medications to calm me down so that in a few days counselors would be able to talk to me.

My husband, Robert, spoke up vehemently in my defense. He said, "you want to put my wife on these meds where the side affect is weight gain? You don't know my wife! You think she is depressed now?" I was a tiny size 6 and that was one thing I was happy about at the time. He knew that if I gained weight that it would devastate me on top of all that I had been through.

Regardless, I was given the meds. I am not a size 6 anymore, but I am mentally well. My time there was short. I stayed a week. The outpatient care lasted two weeks. During my time there and in the outpatient care I felt safe. I was sad when the program ended. I learned a lot about coping and how to change my thinking. Gradually, I was weaned off of the medications.

Since then I have had many months of counseling. I had one counselor tell me that one day I would be talking about this situation as if had happened to someone else, and not me. He said that I would be able to help people like me some day. I didn't believe him. He was right.

I still have times of panic and times of despair as I watch my adult children suffer from their memories of the molestations. They are all adults now and all of them are working through their pain in their own way. I never know what I am going to have to handle concerning their recovery.

I have watched Shelly have flashbacks so severe that she was crawling on the floor and acting out the memory of the abuse. I have watched her twin sister, Karen, age -regress in front of a judge and a court room filled with people. I have watched my oldest son, Paul, have many mental breakdowns. I have called 911 for him. I saw my oldest daughter, Gina, have a flashback while she was in a hospital being treated for cancer. She wanted to pull all the tubes out.

The strength that I have is from the God that I had so much anger towards. I no longer drown myself in alcohol and I am only on a very small dose of anti-anxiety medication. I have to work at being sane, daily; sometimes one second at a time, for I have six adult children who need me.

I am more than a survivor. I decided that I would win over "dirty boy's" plans to destroy me by having a great life! If I didn't have the loving support from my husband, Robert, I probably wouldn't have made it. He never gave up on me. He made me love myself. He made me change the mental lies that were in my brain and accept the fact that Amy is a wonderful person; she was just a victim too.

Since recovering from my last bout of severe depression, I managed to go back to college. I have an Associate's degree in Education with a GPA of 3.96. I am now very close to attaining my Bachelor's degree in Psychology and so far have a GPA of 3.85. I am not stupid. I credit my success to God and to my father's cheering and my husband's support. My plans are to be an Art Therapist for sexually abused children, and for those in the family who were secondary victims like me.

Newly found old friends who understand because they have experienced hellish things in their own lives are helping immensely as well. Thanks to you, my caring friends, I hope that my story will encourage someone and give them hope that there is life after tragedy and that there are possibilities way beyond our greatest imagination for our lives. In sobriety, to anyone out there who is considering suicide as an answer; it isn't the answer, Keep living, it's worth it! I am living proof!

Todd (New Jersey)

I was introduced to alcohol when I was 4 or 5. I would sit in my grandfather's lap while he drank his rye whiskey and soda, and he would give me occasional sips. Turns out, he was the only alcoholic in the family that I know of. I had a relatively happy childhood until I was 9. That was when my dad died and my world turned upside down.

My mom remarried within a year to a guy with 4 children. Counting them, myself, and my brother and sister, there were 9 people crammed into our house. My oldest step-brother began to sexually molest me when I was 10, and my step-father liked to beat up on me. By this time I couldn't trust anyone and I was afraid of everything. I found a friend whose older sister would buy us beer, and drink and smoke weed with us. My step-brother continued to molest me until I was 12. By then I had enough inner strength to be able to say "NO". I began to build a wall up around me so that no one could get in and hurt me anymore.

As I grew up I found myself drinking and drugging more and more. By 16 my favorite "flavor" was Jack Daniels. My inner circle of friends were all stoners. I would try practically any drug that I could get my hands on. That was when I quit school and hung out all day with my best friend Joe and just drank and got high.

At 17, I decided to join the Navy. After boot camp and various schools, I was sent to the pacific fleet in Pearl Harbor, Hawaii. That was where everything changed. Drinking was kind of the "official," unofficial sport when we were off duty, and cocaine was the drug of choice to numb my soul from all the chaos around me. I was warned plenty of times about showing up for duty high or drunk, but I never received any punitive punishment, nor was I sent to "dry dock," which was the Navy's version of rehab. I can't help but wonder what might have been if they'd insisted I go.

When I left the navy at the age of 20, I went back to my old stomping grounds in southern New Jersey and started working as a bartender in Philadelphia. Perfect job for a burgeoning alcoholic. I continued to party without a care in the world until I met my wife to be when I was 26.

We were married 2 years later, but I knew in order to keep her I'd have to stop drinking and drugging. I guess I was so much in love that I was able to put the bottle and the rest of it down. I don't know how I did it, but I stayed clean and sober for the first 12 years of our marriage.

I began to drink on business trips towards the end, but would stay sober at home. My wife and I began to communicate less and less. Sex became a rarity, and it was like 2 roommates sharing a house. Most of the problems were stemming from the depression that I was sliding into deeper by the day. We separated and were divorced after 15 years. We are best friends today. A little strange, huh?

The minute I left my wife and got my own apartment I started drinking again like I had never stopped and my depression continued to deepen. After a couple of weeks you had to wade through the cans and bottles on the floor of my place.

In 2005 I was diagnosed with diabetic peripheral neuropathy. The pain in my hands and feet was continuous and became so bad that my neurologist began prescribing opiate painkillers, dilaudid and fentanyl, and I was in heaven. Of course I continued to drink thinking nothing of mixing alcohol with these potent drugs.

I lost my job as a program director for a major distance education company when I fell asleep during a client meeting I was supposed to be running in 2006. I was fired on the spot, and I haven't worked since. Over the next couple of years I dug myself so far into debt that I had nothing left. Lost the house and the car too.

I ended up living with my mom and her 3rd husband in south Florida. By then the neuropathic pain was so bad I was spending most of my time in bed, and every day was the same. It was kind of like my own personal "groundhog day." The only thing to look forward to was getting to the liquor store and the pharmacy. Not long after I began to beg God to take my life every night, which was kind of funny since I was pissed off at God and blamed him for all the terrible things that had happened to me in my life.

After about a year of living this way, I decided to call it quits. I wasn't going to wait for God to intercede anymore; I was going to do it myself. One night I sucked the juice out of three fentanyl patches, took a big handful of dilaudid, and washed it all down with a quart of vodka. Should've been enough to kill a few people, but somehow I came to about 36 hours later with the worst hangover I'd ever had in my life. My heavy drinking nights usually ended up in blackouts for me, but I remember that one.

At that point the only reason I could come up with for not dying was that God, for some reason, had other plans for me. A few days later my brother called and asked me if I wanted to go to rehab. Not having any other options I could see at that point I said yes, and the next day I was on a plane bound for Malibu, California. That rehab and my brother saved my life!

Brian W. (California) A Poem

Addiction

With a one track mind you'll find it hard to find relaxing time

When your back's always up against the wall and want help but won't call

When you look at all your flaws and feeling dark...looking for your heart

If you feel like you stand out and are unwelcomed and this feeling isn't just seldom

If today feels worse than yesterday and you say "I'd be better in a grave"

If you chip away at yourself until you're just bones, and even your bones are fatigued and weak

If you speak...and when done...you feel you shouldn't have

Here's an antidote...the man who wrote
"Sing Song Blue" didn't write it about you

Accept the smile from the stranger, Then pass it on...now that's the song

Open up and talk to someone...When you're feeling broken up

You'll feel much better...Maybe write yourself a letter

Put in it what you want and use your heart for a fresh start

Give yourself some credit because self-abuse would kill you if you let it

You can't think your way into acting differently. But you can act your way into thinking differently.

"Back home in New Jersey. Hangin' out in my cousin Steve's garage. Still clean and sober." – 2011

PART IV:
SUCCESS STORIES

It's A Rare Wind Don't Blow Somebody some Good.

Cookie (New Jersey)

I met Cookie about a year and a half ago in the south Florida rehab. She was there before me, so I was coming in as she was going out, so to speak. We got to know each other pretty well in the three day overlap of our stays there.

Ironically, we lived near each other in the same small town up north and our conversations were smooth, fun and even intelligent for two people in their fifties, surprisingly finding themselves in rehab for alcohol and drug addiction. After both having fairly successful lives thus far, neither of us had ever dreamed of this situation ever occurring.

But there we were. Both proud of our personal decision to seek professional help for our addictions. Walking into an unknown world with a totally unforeseeable future is no easy task! But you do what you have to do in life. Pretty simple.

One balmy night out at the tables, Cookie lit a cigarette, washed the first drag down with a swig Of black coffee and said, "Ya know Nelson, life may be hard, but the truth makes it easier. Once I started being honest with myself and to the people who are closest to me, it kinda took away some of the power of my addictions. That evil desire to get fucked up all the time seems to have lost its edge. Does that make sense? I said, "Well, hell yes it makes sense! " I'll never forget that night. Cookie and I agreed that more people should muster up the guts and get their asses into a rehab , like we did. Sometimes in life you just do what you have to do. Suck it up...

Well anyway, Cookie called me today to tell me she has been straight for 14 months and loves it. She has a job now with a pretty good company in Miami as a receptionist, and just got a small raise in pay. She also has a guy she kind of likes.

We talked about how good rehab had done for us both and about some of our awesome friends we met down there and will never forget.

I came back to Jersey, but Cookie stayed in south Florida. We made plans for me to come down and visit her within the next few months. She has a two bedroom condo five blocks from the beach and told me that her new "boyfriend" and I would get along great.

Can't wait! I really miss South Florida.

I am so proud of Cookie! She was so totally addicted to alcohol and pain killers that it seemed impossible that she would ever have the strength to break the chains of that horrible disease of addiction.

But she did! God bless ya girl!

Your forever buddy, Nelson.

Pete (Florida)

Fresh out of law school, it really looked like Pete had it goin' on. A good looking kid with a great personality and sense of humor. Everybody liked him and sincerely wished him well on his apparently bright future.

But Pete had a secret. He was a junkie.

A few years back, early in law school, Pete and a couple of his buddies started doing a little speed and coke to help them stay awake longer so they could study. Law school didn't come easy for Pete. He really had to work at it.

And then one night after a long session of studying, Pete picked up a brunette in a local bar. Once back at his place, the sexy brunette gave Pete a 40 mg. oxycontin to try. He had never taken oxys before, but had heard a lot about them. As soon as Pete got that oxy buzz going on, his whole world changed.

He had found his new true love, and it wasn't the girl he'd picked up less than an hour and a half ago at the bar. It was oxys! His oxy habit got so expensive, that even with the decent pay he was receiving as a young lawyer for a medium sized law firm in Juno Beach, Florida, he found it hard to keep up with his habit.

He was going broke, so he did what so many other oxy addicts eventually find themselves doing. He switched from oxys to heroin, which was much cheaper and offered a similar kind of "high".

Early in his recovery at a rehab facility, Pete once said in his morning primary group that, "I'd rather have a pile of oxys than a pile of gold." His therapist told him, "Well, you don't have either, Pete. All you've got is a pile of trouble, the kind that will crush you and kill you, and you know it." Pete replied, "I don't give a fuck anymore. In all honesty, all I need is a couple oxys or a few bags of dope. " He was deadly serious.

That was twelve years ago. At a special Narcotics Anonymous "Rally On The Beach" event, Pete was the special guest speaker, and WOW!, his story and how he presented it was very, very impressive and inspiring. He is now a senior partner at another law firm in West Palm Beach, as well as an inspirational speaker at functions such as the one on the beach last night.

Pete made it clear that the there is definitely life after drugs. Pete demonstrated that clearly and with a lot of class. Everybody wanted to be like him after the meeting. Really cool.

Jon (Oregon)

In my opinion. Jon is no less than a miracle man.

I'll never forget that eerie early morning in the south Florida rehab with the sun just coming up over the Atlantic when Jon walked up to me with a very weird look on his face. Well, as I mentioned earlier in this book, Jon's brother Steve had died a few months earlier and it just so happened that I looked exactly like him. Jon said that Steve and I could have easily passed as twins.

That's when Jon and I started to become friends.

One day Jon said, " Talking to you, it sometimes feels like I'm talking to my brother Steve. You two don't just look alike, you are a lot like him in other ways, too. But hell, this whole journey has been surreal - almost bizarre. Maybe it's just that I'm seeing things in a different light now since getting straight. All I know is that I like it and hope to God I can hold on to it."

Well, I just got some pictures of Jon as well as a letter in the mail. He is now back home in Oregon. He looks great! His pancreas has healed, his diabetes is under control and best of all, he's been clean and sober for 13 months. He has a job as a fork-lift operator and really enjoys the job and the people he works with.

I must say that when I first met Jon, he was in such poor physical health and so badly cross-addicted that I didn't think he would live very long. Man, sure am glad I was wrong about that!

Jon is a good example of having trust in his therapists and following their directions. He still attends AA meetings three times a week in his hometown in Oregon. I e-mailed Jon and thanked him for the letter and pictures. I also mentioned to him that I have always wanted to visit Oregon. Jon said, "Hey buddy, my door is always open for you. Come on out, anytime."

Think I'll take him up on that someday.

Todd (New Jersey)

My detox lasted almost 5 days. They had me taking Suboxone for the opiate withdrawal and for my pain. The rehab guaranteed that they would get me started on the 12 steps, relieve my depression, and get me back on my feet and walking again (I have peripheral neuropathy). At first I said, "yeah, sure" but they did!

It took 112 days before I was ready to leave on the next leg of my journey. Many life changing things happened to me in rehab. My therapist was a really awesome woman named Nancy, and she helped me overcome some tremendous baggage that I'd always carried around with me from earlier in life. One of those momentous things was my change in attitude about God and spirituality.

Religion means nothing more to me than ritual, culture, and dogma, but spirituality has since become a foundation of my life. I can now walk in the grace of my Higher Power. Prayer and meditation on a daily basis keep me close to Him.

One day early in my rehab stay, one of the counselors, Barbara, who had been promising to give me a tour of the property via a golf cart ride (because I still was in great pain when on my feet) said, "Come on, let's do it." During our ride around the property I ended up pouring out my heart and telling her most of my story.

Of course, being the unique alcoholic and addict that I am, I always believed that my story was worse than yours, and most everyone else's too. Well, Barbara told me her story and she blew me away. Her story was like a horror movie come to life. It really humbled me to think that I'd thought "I'd had it so bad" all those years. We then started to talk about spiritually and she helped me start on the path of finding "the God of my understanding."

Another of the folks from the local AA community (which by the way was awesome), Joanie, taught me the Serenity Prayer. She told me that I could "re-start my day" if I was having difficulties any time I wanted just by saying it.

While I'm certainly not proud of this fact, fear had been the one of the few emotions in my life that I could actually feel. I'd spent the last 35 odd years trying to numb out every single one of the little fuckers, but fear mostly ruled my days, and especially my nights. It was so strong it felt like a choke hold around my neck.

Well, one day about 3 weeks after my ride with Barbara and taking Joanie's advice I was talking with another counselor, Becky, about fear and I realized that for the first time in what seemed like forever I wasn't afraid of what was going to happen to me. I wasn't choking on the fear. I was actually happy.

It had been so long since I felt true happiness that wasn't from being buzzed, that at first I didn't recognize it for what it was. Since I've gotten sober, I am able to feel and be in touch with my emotions for perhaps the first time since I was a child. And it's not just the good ones. The painful and destructive ones shine right on through as well.

But now I wouldn't have it any other way. I'd gone from suicidal to feeling what it's really like to be alive (and wanting to stay that way) in just a couple of months. I now have more than 2 years clean & sober.

My higher power and the program and fellowship of AA have given me a way to not only stay sober, but to live my life head on. I have an AA sponsor and a home group and I work the 12 steps. I take service commitments regularly by hosting meetings in rehabs and institutions, being an elected representative of my group, or simply by making the coffee or greeting people at the door of a meeting as they arrive — anything I can do to "get out of my head." The AA promises are beginning to come true for me.

I don't have to avoid troubles anymore, nor do I have difficulty with my relationships. I am living life on life's terms.

I'm still not working, but after a 4 year long battle with the Social Security Administration, I recently got my disability. Man, gettin' money (or even a letter in the mail) out of those guys is like pulling teeth! I am returning to school to pursue a graduate degree in psychology or social work. Like so many other adults who were traumatized as children, I'd eventually like to work with and help children who have been abused.

I have no regrets because everything I've gone through in my life has shaped me into who I am today.

Unfortunately I had to try to kill myself before I got the help I needed, but as I said earlier, "God had other plans."

I think I'll try his way for a change.

Owen (Florida)

If it hadn't been for all of the trials and tribulations I've had to overcome over this past year, and the incredible people I've met and gotten to know, I would have looked at Owen as just another less than perfect human being trying to make it through this jagged journey called life.

But after rooming with him for a few months in a half-way house in South Florida I saw the goodness in Owen. The uniqueness. We would sit out in front of our apartment and talk about our families, sports, politics, religion, you name it.

And we never even had one argument, although we didn't always agree. True friends. Owen was a hard-core alcoholic and crack-head. He'd been through hell and was now trying to get right with God and with himself. He hated what he had become.

The rehab we had just come from convinced Owen that he had a lot to live for. A lot to stay sober for. His therapist, Loretta, was awesome and later told me that she knew he would make it and stay sober. She was right.

He is still in the half-way house and has a part time job at the rehab as a groundskeeper and maintenance helper. His plans are to take courses and become a drug counselor or personnel tech at the rehab facility.

All of his counselors and therapists think he's got what it takes. So do I.

Owen always used to say to the new people coming into rehab, " Hey, if I can get clean and stay clean, anybody can. My addiction had me by the balls, so I had to make a run for it. Sure, It hurt like all hell at first. But I've still got my balls and luckily, now I have my brains back too. So can you. Go for it! "

HOW TO SMILE

Chaos and confusion

Are the by-products

Of fear and self

Victimization

Wild dogs

Snapping at the conscious

Tiger sharks circling

The heart, backing off

When the determination to hate

Takes a shower, changes

Clothes and steps out

Into the day with

The clean desire to heal

For Julie.

PART V:
EPILOGUE

Nelson (New Jersey)

Day 275 – 4:00pm

"As I sit here in the sand on the Gold coast of southeast Florida, I am in the process of making another huge decision. Lord, there have been so many over the past few months, give me strength."

Should I leave the comforting shade of the Palm tree I am lounging under, the warmth of the ocean, the great fishing and the endearing friends I have made here, and return to New Jersey and my family?

This beach is now my home and I'm almost afraid to leave this paradise. The peace I feel here is held strong in what I can only describe as the tender hands of fate.

Gazing out across the turquoise water, in my mind I cannot help but glance into the rear-view mirror of my life, and New Jersey appears as a car-wreck with shards of shattered glass and twisted metal strewn across some hideous roadway. My addictions and the mayhem that ensued had taken its destructive toll.

No, I do not want to leave my new home and return to New Jersey, but my Daughter and Grandson are there and they have a much stronger allure for me than even a Miami sunrise. And I must go back and clear the roadway. Or at least try. I've learned to take nothing for granted and just follow my heart.

So now I've decided. I must go back to my roots and return to New Jersey. Case closed. I'll order my plane ticket as soon as I return to my waterfront haven on Hendricks Isle. *Gee, I love that place.* But, that's how I roll these days. I make a decision and promptly act on it. I live one day at a time with the confidence that God will lead my way. Rehab helped me take that approach and it has been working for me so far.

I have no idea where I am going after my plane lands in Atlantic City, or how I'm going to get 'home,' 40 miles west of the airport. The home I shared with my wife of 32 years I can no longer return to. And I refuse to impose myself on my daughter and her family. Hell, I can't even sleep in my car or truck. My wife owns the car and I sold my truck as well as my two boats before I admitted myself into the first rehab.

But something magical will happen. I'll land on my feet again. Of that I have faith. Sure enough, a dear friend and former neighbor of mine in my hometown of Millville offered to pick me up at the airport, his daughter had a nice room I could rent and he took me out to buy a car with the couple of grand I had been able to save up down in paradise. *Thanks man. You know who you are.*

Now all I wanted to do is hop on that plane and hug my Daughter, Dana Marie and my Grandson, Carter Samuel. It's been months since I have seen them and I know it might be an awkward reunion, after all, she has seen the accident on that roadway of her Daddy's addictions. The roadway I am coming home to repair.

Day 1,000 – 7:05am

Coffee's on, and with my dog Bree at my side, I light a
cigarette and call my daughter who is just a few days
away from delivering into the world my second
Grandson. His name will be Preston Jay. I can't wait to
meet him!

I'll tell you; these last one thousand days have been more than a journey. It has felt more like an epic novel spanning centuries all crammed into a thousand days of constant change, stress, pain, heartbreak and miraculous transformation. And as the main character in this sometimes macabre, sometimes glorious sojourn, I feel beaten down and at the same time lifted up.

The little cabin in the woods that I share with my mixed breed companion, Bree, is but a few miles from my Daughter's home. My son lives in Los Angeles and we talk and e-mail nearly every day. He is soon to be married to a lovely girl and between sips of coffee, brings a smile to my face.

Things are coming together, and though it took two years for me to get over the tragedy of my shattered marriage, the sun is coming up over the trees, the birds are singing and I am clean and sober. I consider this my new life, and though I struggled painfully hard to reclaim my old one, God had other plans. Isn't it funny how He always knows what's best?

I can only say that I am finally happy again. My first book, the one you just read is doing well and hopefully helping people to face their demons head-on and defeat them. I am now working on my second book titled, "Raven April", a psychological thriller, a fictional novel I hope you will all read when I'm finished. I am still in constant lower back, hip and leg pain, but I have learned to deal with it without the aid of prescription painkillers. I battled that awful demon and won. And as I've often said, "I know you can too."

9:42 am — Well, it's time to fill the bird feeder and the bird bath. Bree wants to be fed and scratched, I need to do a load of wash and take a shower. Later, I will be getting back to work on my new book in progress. Wish me luck on that? Thanks.

Now it's my turn to thank each and every one of you for reading this book. I truly hope and pray that you will take away a feeling of hope, happiness and faith. If it wasn't for the belief in my Higher Power, the therapists, as well as AA and NA, I wouldn't be writing to you right now. Truth be told, I would probably be dead. But because of whipping the disease of addiction, I am here. And I am delighted that you are too.

There is supposed to be a full moon tonight, So after this day is done, and the sun sets over the Delaware Bay, I'll sit outside with Bree, look up at the moon and give thanks for another day well lived. Day 1,001, here I come!

What I've Learned

- I've learned that addiction is a disease.

- I've learned that addiction can be conquered in some and controlled in others.

- I've learned that there is black and white and that there is gray, too.

- I've learned that addicts and alcoholics are, for the most part, good people. Special.

- I've learned that NA and AA can work if you work it.

- I've learned that addiction can rip hearts out.

- I've learned that rehabs and therapists are God's blessing.

- I've learned to accept my losses, existence and fate.

- I've learned to face my past.

- I've learned to stay close to God's word.

- I've learned to forgive myself and others as well.

- I've learned to believe in Angels. And demons.

- I've learned how to be strong when needed.

- I've learned how and why to be humble.

- I've learned that Love and family are more precious than riches.

- I've learned that God knows us all and loves us all.

"Looking at a bright new horizon." – 2012

Afterword

I Hope and pray that my book has helped you understand the diseases of drug addiction and alcoholism a little better. They are both huge problems in our society today. I would like to add that in no way should any of my doctors who prescribed me the much needed pain and anti-anxiety medication following my accident be held responsible for my acquired dependency upon them. Neither they nor I could have predicted my reaction to them.

Please try and be compassionate and understanding when dealing with those of us who have been ensnared by this brutal affliction.

Remember, there is always hope and people who are ready to help when their journey into darkness has brought them to the welcoming door of recovery. Encourage anyone you know to seek help. They can start by calling the National Substance Abuse Hotline at: 800-662-HELP (800-662-4357) to find an AA or NA meeting, or a list of rehabs in their area.

Sincerely,

Nelson John Trout

Rest In Peace

John Belushi	Janis Joplin	Elvis Presley
Len Bias	Dorothy Killgallen	Freddie Prinze
Truman Capote	John Kordic	Dee Dee Ramone
Montgomery Clift	Alan Ladd	Johnny Ray
Kurt Cobain	Barbara La Marr	Rachel Roberts
Dorothy Dandridge	Heath Ledger	David Ruffin
Tommy Dorcey	Bela Lugosi	George Sanders
Brian Epstein	Frankie Lyman	Hillel Slovak
Chris Farley	Marilyn Monroe	Anna Nicole Smith
WC Fields	Keith Moon	Inger Stevens
Sigmund Freud	Jim Morrison	Rory Storm
Judy Garland	Christina Onassis	Margaret Sullivan
Andy Gibb	Charlie Parker	Dylan Thomas
Bobby Hatfield	Gram Parsons	Ike Turner
Margaux Hemmingway	Chris Penn	Sid Vicious
Jimi Hendrix	Papa John Phillips	Gene Vincent
Billie Holiday	River Phoenix	Dinah Washington
Howard Hughes	Rob Pilatus	Keith Whitley
Phyllis Hyman	Dana Plato	Dennis Wilson
Michael Jackson	Jackson Pollock	Hank Williams
Brian Jones	Darrell Porter	Amy Winehouse

This list is just a tiny portion of the millions of human beings who have succumbed to the heartless disease of addiction. I was almost one of them. So, I beg of you, please reach out and get help before you are written into this list. Get into rehab; it's frightening, I know, I've been there. But that decision saved my life. It can save yours, too.

Sincerely and With Love,

Nelson John Trout